THE
LAUNDRY LIST:
A Mom's Guide to Running a
Successful Business and Home

BY
RACHEL BRENKE

You really have no idea what you can pull off until it is sink or swim time.

To NEB and the Tres Amigos.

TABLE OF CONTENTS

INTRODUCTION

Don't even start thinking that this book is going to solve all your problems. It's not. But don't put it back on the shelf! The tips in here come out of some very hard learned lessons. You know the phrase "survival of the fittest?" That couldn't be truer than a "single mom" (read: husband deployed all the time) with three kids, working on a doctorate and building multiple businesses. This girl right here. I am often asked exactly how I manage it all and still…survive. So here you go. No holds barred. Going to show you all exactly how to manage it, survive and even have time to get those grass stains out of the soccer uniform…all before dinner!

***

An important thing to realize is that each business owner's goals are different. Some aspects of these tips will be much harder hitting to one person than the next. It is all going to depend on exactly what your professional and personal goals are. Even more important to remember is that if you make it through the day, customers are happy (or at least somewhat happy), and the children are alive, then you have succeeded.

***

Keep in mind through the entire book my number one goal is to be able to give as much to my family and customers without sacrificing either to a detriment. Family always should come first.

***

So why am I here to write this for you? Because I wish I had found someone with trials and struggles to break it all down for me. Open up for me. To show me the way. So here I am mistakes and all. I started out on my journey to owning a business before I even knew what type of business I would get into. I remember researching and being so overwhelmed with the Internet resources. I didn't know where to turn or where to go. I was in this mindset that all resources on the web were geared toward experienced business owners. They were there to help already existing owners get larger and make more money. I just wanted to get set up. I remember turning to my husband and saying to him "One day I want a business where I help non-profits and for-profits get set up online." In a round about way, here I am.

My desire for this website and business started during my undergraduate years with one child at home. I went on to pursue real estate and my Masters in Business Administration while I mulled over the idea of law school. With a two-year old at home and a husband constantly gone with the Army, I was unsure how it would all turn out. That year I was diagnosed with thyroid cancer, of which I am still in remission for. That was the last straw. I wanted to make a difference. I wanted to be a business owner.

While pursuing the MBA, I continued to maintain three online apparel stores I had set up during my undergraduate years. It wasn't fancy, and still isn't fancy. But it provided a car payment or two a month. The most important part was that I was able to learn marketing and business skills while still having the care of a website platform to provide distribution and payment channels. I also was able to start consulting by helping others start up their businesses. Consulting was small scale, as I was learning myself for web-based business; but I was able to help brick and mortar businesses move forward with formation.

While I continued to build these businesses through social media, my MBA ended and it was time to make a decision. Law school or not? My husband had just returned from deployment number 3 to Iraq and we still only had one child. I decided to go for it. Even though it meant moving across the country with one child in tow and leaving the husband behind. Plus, we would soon find out I was pregnant with our second (the Olivia who makes a few appearances in this book).

Everyone called me crazy.

And they still kind of do...every day.

So I found myself across country from husband, with a three year old, pregnant and in my first year of law school. Oh yeah...let's not forget the three online apparel stores as well. Some friends and family went as far as to insistently talk me out of pursuing law school at that time. Of course, this drove me harder. I think this was the turning point in learning how to sink or swim. Without the pivotal moment of deciding to pursue law school and the business despite other circumstances, I wouldn't be here writing this book. That first year is also when I began my photography business with what my husband affectionately refers to as the "worst Christmas present ever". Mostly because I never get the camera out of his face.

Time went on. The first year of law school ended and we then had two children. He deployed to Iraq for the fourth time. #1, #2 and I were still living across the country from where we were stationed. By the time my husband came home a year later, I had made arrangements to move our little family back together. I made arrangements to finish law school in another state, moved my quickly-built thriving photography business to another state, and then found out we were pregnant with #3 the same month I was to graduate and begin the studying for the bar.

I pretty much dedicated my last year of law school to making it. I was not going to give in now. Consulting had exploded, the apparel stores were steady, and photography was exceeding my original goals. Blogging, newsletters, Skype calls and legal research had become my life. All while having three kids and a husband gone. It was just a normal day to spend the long hours and dedicated time to get it all accomplished.

All of this is to show that I **had** to make it. I had to do it because some thought I couldn't. I wanted to make it for those who knew I could. I had to adapt. It was sort of an evolutionary time learning to take care of myself, my kids, school and the businesses. I still found time to exercise, spend time with the kids and succeed in all areas.

In order to do that, I had to wash laundry. I had to keep whites white and colors intact.

This is my laundry list of secrets.

CHAPTER ONE:

SETTING UP SHOP

O h, man! The million dollar question, to jump in the crazy pool of owning your own business or not? It is kind of like deciding to have kids. I think some people believe they are ready, but have no idea. Some people will never be ready. Just like the doctor didn't hand you a how-to manual when he handed you Little Timmy, there really isn't a precise manual to guide you along. The best you can do is to learn from those who have been there (cough...me...) and haven't drowned (yet).

Running a business IS a lot like parenting.

Trial and error. There is never a clear cut answer.

Running a business, like having kids, involves a lot of tears and vomit along the way...then there are the customers. I'm only kidding...sort of. It is a lot of hard work. More work than this little book probably can tell you, but my goal is to break it down and help you get on the right path. If you're picking up this book because you've already jumped into the crazy pool, then good for you! This chapter may serve as a good refresher and I may even throw in a few curve balls you may not have thought about. If you haven't taken the plunge but are thinking about it, then let's figure out if running your own business is right for you!

***

SHOULD I BE MY OWN BOSS?

It is kind of scary to think that you are the boss, huh? You're not only the boss; you will also be the secretary, lunch gofer, coffee maker, donut picker upper, marketing manager, accountant…and the list goes on. Obviously, as we will get to, you can outsource some of these, but if you're starting barebones without much of a business structure or financial investment there probably isn't much option other than to juggle all these roles.

Questions to ask before jumping in:

- Do I want to take on all those roles?
- What is my financial situation for investment?
- Do I have any idea how to actually run a business?
- Does my family depend on this money?
- What is my goal for starting my own business? Entrepreneurship? Staying home with the kids? Independence?

***

WHY SHOULD I GET LEGIT?

The easy answer? Because it's the right thing to do. Besides that, there are other benefits including avoiding fines, maintaining your reputation, cultivating networking relationships, tax deductions and offering credibility to your customers.

Laundry Tip: In some states you can be fined up to $500 a DAY for every day that you operate as a business but are not legit. Do it.

***

SO I WANT TO OPEN MY BUSINESS. NOW WHAT?

Deciding to open a business is a daunting and overwhelming task. It sort of works this way....if it's not a teensy bit scary then you're probably circling the wrong block or are just crazy! Even the most solid business person will feel some angst because it is their livelihood and craft being put on the line and out into the world. Knowing the ways to properly get legit (such as through formation and taxes) will reduce the angst and help set you on a path for success.

Laundry Tip: Don't rush into it. Jumping in merely because you're inspired can damage your taste for entrepreneurship before it gets off the ground.

We need to examine business structures, taxes and other various licenses. When in doubt, call your local small business agency or appropriate governmental agency. You'd be surprised how helpful they can be and at the amount of information that is put out for small business owners (i.e. my blog is one!). If you get a not-so-helpful employee at one of these agencies, hang up and call again later – pray you get someone else. But before calling, you could take a gander at the rest of this chapter for business structures and other tips to give you a framework!

***

WHAT BUSINESS STRUCTURES ARE AVAILABLE TO ME?

There are a variety of business structures to choose from including Sole Proprietor, Limited Liability Company (LLC), and Corporation. Choosing the structure depends on the type of business, initial investment cost, personal choice of liability, and tax liability. Each has their own way to be set up, along with individual pros and cons.

Sole Proprietor

Sole proprietorships are often the most popular with newest small business owners that have minor monetary investment to work with. These are often created through filing a "doing business as" certificate with the state or county. While a sole proprietorship has the easiest and lowest investment cost, the tradeoff is that sole proprietorships do not offer liability protection. As the owner of a sole proprietorship, personal assets are not shielded and separate from the business assets. For taxation, a sole proprietor simply files a Schedule "C" with personal income tax returns.

Set Up: Some states require only a DBA (doing business as) and some require nothing! It depends on your locale.

Limited Liability Company

A second type of business structure is that of a limited liability company (LLC). This structure offers liability protection for the owner because business and personal assets are deemed separate. While LLC's have a greater initial monetary investment accompanying the filing of the Articles of Organization when forming the company, this structure is most beneficial to business owners because of the liability protection and flexibility of tax planning. All LLC earnings are taxed only once because all income, deductions, losses and credits "flow through" to the owners of the company. LLC's are can be managed by members, managers, or a hybrid. In an LLC the income, losses, deductions and credits may be divided up through proper documentation.

Set Up: For the most part, these are set up by filing the Articles of Organization. The fees of LLC's range greatly, some with great initial startup costs, others with reoccurring renewal fees.

Laundry Tip: An LLC is a great way to break into the business field at a decently low monetary investment but obtains liability protection upon formation. This is especially important for parents with children and personal assets.

Corporations

Corporations round up the most popular business structures for small businesses. Corporations, like LLC's, require a bit more intensive start-up investment and paperwork filing than sole proprietorships but have benefits of their own. There are two types of corporations: C and S corporations. While C corporations may be subject to double taxation, they can be avoided if owners working in the business earn a reasonable standard of salary. Also, if your intention is to be a publicly traded company, this is the business structure to select. The second type is that of an S corporation. This is the more popular business structure choice out of the two corporations; however, unlike with the LLC structure, profits cannot be unevenly distributed through agreement and the corporation is subject to state corporate fees.

Laws to form the chosen business structure vary by state but have the same baseline advantages and disadvantages. Examining long-term goals for the business and balancing these goals with present income investment, you can make an educated decision for your business. The most important thing to note is that business structures may be changed through additional filings and monetary investments to the state of formation.

To set up a corporation will depend upon the type and a few select items. While an attorney is advised for all business structures, it is definitely imperative to consult an attorney when setting up a Corporation, as there are many ins and outs because the tax code is forever changing.

***

HOW DO I KNOW WHICH BUSINESS STRUCTURE I WANT?

Rank these factors from most important to least important to help you decide on structure.

- Desired protection of assets

- Monetary investment

- Renewals

- Long term goals

Then come back and refer to the pros/cons listed above in each type. This should give you an idea of which business structure is most appropriate for your needs and for the type of business you plan to operate.

***

WHAT DO I DO ABOUT TAXES?

First STOP! Anytime someone talks about taxes, we need to distinguish which type. There are three major types of taxes to keep in mind when running a business: (1) Federal Income Tax, (2) State Income Tax, (3) State Sales Tax. There are other miscellaneous taxes but those are business formation and jurisdiction specific, so let's stick with these as a baseline.

- Federal Income Tax

Federal income tax is on your INCOME. There is no federal sales tax, as that is a state driven thing (see #3 State sales tax). This is your responsibility to claim yearly during the dreaded tax time! It is suggested that you save a portion of your income throughout the year so that you're not surprised at tax time when you get a bill from the IRS. Why would you get a bill? Think about it! When you are employed by a "real employer," they have you fill out withholdings forms and hold the money FOR you.

When you run your own business and play accountant, you must do your own withholdings! Note: Always check with the IRS to see your options for paying throughout the year.

- State Income Tax

This is very similar to federal income tax, except it is at the state level! Not too hard, right? You will want to withhold enough to cover your state income tax as well as the federal.

- State Sales Tax

If you have a business and are selling products, you are required to collect sales tax for your state. All jurisdictions vary on what services and products are taxed, so be sure to always consult a tax attorney or the taxing agency. Don't fret; this isn't coming out of YOUR pocket. It is to be applied on top of your prices to your customers. You're merely the middleman.

Sales tax permits are easy to get through the state and are often free to obtain. Even if you have no customers for a taxable period, you must still file a sales tax return and input ZERO, or you'll get hit with a late fee!

Sales tax permits are generally free to get from your state – some states do require you to pay. But either way, why not do it? Not to mention, it is the right (and legal) thing to do!

Laundry Tip: This is an area of business that outsourcing has a great return on investment. Peace of mind. Accuracy.

***

WHAT IF I SELL DIGITAL PRODUCTS?

Ahh...the ever changing tax code and the intricacies of dealing with digital products. Some states classify digital products as subject to sales tax while others do not. Always consult your taxing agency and/or an attorney.

***

WHAT TYPES OF LEGAL DOCUMENTS DO I NEED TO PROTECT MYSELF?

Always consult an attorney for the state that you are engaging in business and/or your formation state (because they may vary) to determine whether you have all the appropriate legal forms in order.

Contracts are so commonplace in business today that there is no reason not to use one.

***

WHAT IF I'M ALREADY A LEGIT BUSINESS?

It never hurts to run down the checklist above to make sure you have all your legal ducks in a row. Insert into your work routine (and calendar) a time for checking up on new local regulations and renewal dates. Examine if there are any formational changes you want to make. Some questions to ask yourself include:

- Has my business financial situation changed?

- What are my new 1 year and 5 year goals?

- Have I had any life changes that affect the business?

- Have I (or do I) intend on hiring any employees?

***

AFTER READING ALL THIS I'M STILL NOT SURE I'M READY TO GO INTO BUSINESS. HOW DO I KNOW?

This is a question I receive in my inbox on a regular basis. My typical response is "it depends," and I know that doesn't satisfy the reader who is awaiting a response. Do I still squirm at the thought of calling myself a small business owner? You betcha! Here are a few things that I personally believe should be evaluated and achieved prior to entering on the scene as a "professional."

The first aspect to examine is if your business requires a specific licensure or certification. If so, then this is the first step in a regulated industry. By law you are not able to engage in business as a certain professional without the proper credentials. However, if you are entering into an industry that has no requirement of licensure or credentials, there may not be a real set timeline. Some business owners achieve benchmarks quicker than others on the path to setting up a business.

Other aspects to evaluate, whether credentials are required or not, include proficiency and consistency of product/service, adequate supports, understanding cost of doing business and the proper business formation.

- Proficiency and Consistency –
  To properly provide a product or service, you must be able to run a business and either create a product or deliver a service with proficiency that your market expects.

- Adequate Channels and Supports
  To be able to deliver the product or service, you must have adequate delivery channels and supports for customer service.

- Understanding Cost of Doing Business.
  This is such a big one. Do you know your true cost of doing business? This is more of personal one. If you don't know, you're going to undervalue your services and will get burned out. Why would you want to do that before even getting off the ground?

- Proper Business Formation –
  See the previous discussion. No illegal businesses. No matter what.

Business requires a startup dedication of time, money and energy. By telling yourself that you are putting the funds back into the business so it's "legit" without reporting is still not legit (with exceptions that are beyond the scope of this post). Don't get caught. Not only do I think it is wrong, but it could potentially destroy your business before it's really off the ground. I'm not stating that these are the be-all and end-all requirements to being a small business owner – just a few things that I have learned along the way.

We never stop growing, but having the foundation of the items above is going to set you up for success more than not having them. I want everyone to succeed. Competition facilitates growth. Helping each other facilitates a better industry.

Don't let obstacles get in your way.

Develop a game plan.

These are just the bare minimums to starting a business. Take from this and build on it!

CHAPTER TWO:

BUSINESS PLANNING

O kay, now onto the goals! You need to have an end goal in sight in order to know the path you're going to take. We're going to start with a crash course on business and marketing planning so you can jot down a few goals to keep in mind as you move through the book. It helps to know these off hand so when you read an efficiency measure or organizational tip, you can formulate your plan of action right then!

So, planning your goals. It's kind of like this…you see a pin on Pinterest and what is the first thing you see? A picture of the end product. You pin it with the full intention of creating it, but then never look at the tutorial or come back to actually do the project. What good will that do you or Little Timmy who wants the Yoda cupcake toppers for his birthday party? No good at all. So break this down as it applies to your business. Each business owner has in their mind an idea of where they want to be. Simply thinking of this and not putting the goal on paper or into practice the steps to reach it will make you about as close to success as those five hundred projects pinned to your board right now. Just like pinning, with your business it is identified that is the product you want to create.

So start there and work backwards by clicking into the tutorial…or in this instance, creating a tutorial for yourself. The goals you plan should be realistic, flexible, come from an educated understanding of the current fiscal health of your business and be written down.

***

BUSINESS PLANNING

A business plan is the tutorial a business owner needs to be successful. For moms, it is the lifeline to ensure you're not spinning your wheels with no forward motion. Being that business owners are more than likely in business to make an income, the goal should start with the desired profit you want to derive out of your business.

First, who are you? What is your business? Seriously, who are you and what are you doing here? Oh, right…business planning. Well, we can't start that without having a firm grasp of the description of your business, market challenges you face, geographic location of your competition, and foreseeable obstacles.

- A description of your business:

    o What services/products do you offer?
    o What is your mission?
    o How are you important to the community?

- A description of your market or business environment:

    o Are there sections of your target market that are underserved and will your services fill that void? If so, write a brief explanation of what this

market is like and how your services are going to get the attention of the customer.
- o Does the market want or value your services? Why or why not?
- o Is there enough money to be made with your services in your target market?
- o How much of a profit will you need to make for your business to pay off?

- Does your business benefit from any distinct marketing advantages?

  - o Is your name already well known?
  - o Do you have high customer loyalty?
  - o Do the local trade organizations endorse your services?

- The marketing challenges you face:

  - o Do you lack brand recognition?
  - o Do you face a limited budget?
  - o Is lack of experience going to present a marketing problem?

- The current geographic location of your competition:

  - o Does the competition within this market leave room for you to be competitive?
  - o Is your intended geographic location a positive or a negative?

- What are your competition's weaknesses? How can you use those weaknesses to your advantage?

      o Does your competition's failure to provide flexible service give you an area you can exploit?

      o Does the competition ignore the local market?

      o Is your competition only focused on high profit areas of business?

- Are there any other foreseeable outside influences on your business?

Second, let's move forward with an overarching goal. Where do you see your business down the road? What is the end goal? Some business owners just have target fiscal benchmarks to meet at a certain timeframe. Others are seeking to build a business to be sold off to a larger company or owner. A few even want to build themselves to be the bigger company that is acquiring smaller companies beneath it. It is important to keep all these things in mind, because as we move into marketing planning you will need to keep your eye on this to ensure your route is taking you to your final destination.

Questions to consider include:

- Where do you want to be in 12 months? 36 months? 72 months?

- What is your desired income?

- What is your desired customer quantity level?

- What is your product sales level?

Third, what is your mission for your business? This isn't the ooey –gooey section that goes on your website or pamphlets. Example: "I sell X product because I love it and I know you need it." Stop. No. This isn't late night television. This is an internal mission statement to guide yourself and your employees (if any) of how to act and what actions the business will be taking in order to fulfill the goals listed. For example, your goal may be to sell out eventually and turn a profit on the sale. That is a goal. A mission would be what you're going to provide customers to build the business to get to that goal, the sellable stage.

I cannot reiterate enough how much a mission statement will make or break your motivation. If you don't have a set mission/goal, you will flounder. Think about what you want to achieve and how you want to achieve it. Jot ideas down before trying to draft the statement. There is no limit (minimum or maximum) to this. This may not seem like a lot, but developing one is harder than you think. You need to incorporate your mission statement into your market (stemming from your market research in your market planning section) and products/services that you will provide.

Questions to ask in mission statement development:

- What do you hope to accomplish with your efforts?

- How do you plan to accomplish these goals?

- For whose benefit does your business exist?

After Development Ask These:

- Is the statement realistic?

- Is it clear and concise?

- Does it demonstrate commitment or is it merely a means to an end?

- Is the statement powerful and motivating?

Examples:

#1

Goal: To reach $500k gross by 2015 and brand the business to be sellable to a private buyer by 2017.

Mission Statement: Profitable growth and brand recognition through stellar quality, superior customer service and commitment to excellence.

#2

Goal: To provide X product to the Tri-State area that is readily available and affordable to the common consumer. The yearly product sales include XX units and will reach a yearly gross amount of $750k by 2017.

Mission Statement: To acquire statewide distribution channels and deliver the product at competitive prices.

Fourth, what is your strategy to get to these goals and fulfill this mission? What is special about you, your business and your product/service? This portion will tie in with the market planning section below. Identify your specific strengths and see how to include these with the product you're selling to your customer base.

Finally, identify the financial health of the business. Health will often depend on whether a business is new or existing. Thriving or floundering. Include all current debts and expenditures. All costs of doing business (CODB) should also be outlined. Costs of doing business include the following:

- Product Cost
- Savings

- Utilities (Internet, Electricity, Phone)
- Rent/Mortgage
- Items used every day to run the business
- Insurance (liability, equipment, health)
- Web Hosting
- Postage/Shipping supplies
- Professional Development
- Subscriptions
- Professional Dues
- Webhosting
- Taxes and Licenses

It is easiest to identify these costs as one yearly amount so you have an overall yearly amount to deduct from gross numbers to find your net.

***

MARKETING PLANNING

Now that you have your baseline goals, it is time to balance your goals against your market. Large companies spend millions upon millions of dollars on market research. Marketing touches every aspect of your business's operation. It is a series of activities designed to identify customer needs and wants, and to satisfy these while making a reasonable profit on a quality product or service. These activities include market research and analysis, product development, pricing, advertising, promotions, publicity, sales and customer service. Developing a marketing plan is one of the most important things you can do to ensure that your business will make a profit.

There are six basic reasons for developing a marketing plan:

- It forces you to identify your target market.

- It forces you to think about both short and long-term marketing strategies.

- It looks at your business as a whole and ties together market objectives.

- It allocates limited resources to create the greatest return.

- It provides a guide to measure progress and outcome.

- It gives clarity to who does what, when, with what marketing tools.

Developing a marketing plan, like business planning, can be a pain. And why shouldn't it be? Your marketing plan is an essential element of your business plan. Every marketing plan should include market research, your mission statement (which is already done!), identified and selected pricing strategies, the definition of your business, and your identified target customer.

Market Research

Market research is simply finding out your customers' desires and needs, as well as figuring out what you can do to satisfy these and still turn a profit. This is done through research and the analysis of said research. Most entrepreneurs believe that market research and analysis is something that only marketing professionals and statisticians are able to do. This is not the case. Marketing research is simply an orderly, objective way of learning about your potential customers and your competition.

Marketing research doesn't have to be complex and expensive. Moreover, it is not a perfect science; it deals with people and their constantly changing likes and dislikes, which can be affected by hundreds of influences, many of which simply cannot be identified.

- Primary Research

  This is the hands-on and body contact research method. Get out and ask people about your business. Gauge their responses and their reactions. This can be done through formal surveys by professional marketing firms, or by informally placing questions out to your customer base. Tools for this research method include direct mail questionnaires, social media surveys, and customer follow-up inquiries.

Laundry Tip: Look to local colleges or business schools that are seeking opportunities for their students to do primary marketing research.

- Secondary Research

  This research is hands off of the customers and hands-on to already published books and surveys. This information is analyzed in light of your business goals and mission (aha! I told you these would come back up!) There are many sources of secondary research material. You can find it in libraries, universities and colleges, trade and general business

***

CREATING A RESEARCH DOC

At this point, you should begin a running document of your market plan and an additional document with your research. Maintaining a research document helps you compile all the information that is uncovered, and also provides a foundation for making future business and market decisions. By crafting a research document out of results from the above market research, the time needed to create the final marketing plan is majorly decreased. This will leave you more time for icing the cupcakes for Little Sally's end-of-year ballet party. Moreover, the research document will be a useful tool in the daily operations of the business. This should be a fluid document with information included and amended as the business grows, market demands shift and your goals change shape.

The first section of the research document should include the competition. This is the real meat of a marketing plan as this will identify pricing points, marketing techniques adapted by competitors and will bring to light potential marketing opportunities not yet tapped into by competition. It is time to act like Harriet the Spy, without the geeky shoes and torn up notebook. Watch your competition's pricing, marketing types and customer feedback.

- Direct Competition

    A direct competitor is a business that produces a like product with similar quality and price point. This competitor is also targeting your target customer.

- Indirect Competition

    This competition is made up of external influences such as cultural, legal, economic, and educational road bumps to customers purchasing your products or services.

Include the following information in your research doc:

- Identify the top three to five direct competitors in your market

- Determine your similarities and differences to these competitors' strengths and weaknesses.

- Are your competitors' weaknesses opening up an untapped area for you to jockey your business into?

- Are your competitors' strengths so strong there is no room for you to run with them?

- Determine whether the direct competitors' business is increasing, decreasing or is maintaining the status quo.

- Identify methods for making your operation more prominent in the community than your competitors' businesses.

- Compare your marketing techniques with these competitors.

- Identify three to five indirect competitors.

Laundry Tip: Appearances can be deceiving! Just because someone appears successful does not necessarily mean they are!

The second section of the research document should be dedicated to identifying your target customer. Remember, there are other people in life besides the one currently pulling on your leg with a runny nose asking for more orange juice. Yes, there are real people out there, and your target customer is one of them! In this part of the research document, you can include a simple list of information about your customer, some basic demographic information and some more detailed information as it relates to your services, such as:

- Who are they?

- What do they want?

- What motivates them to use your services?

- How much monetary value do they place on your products/services?

- What are their demographics? Age? Gender? Socio-economic status?

- How does this customer normally obtain similar products or services?

- Does this customer have any other specific characteristics?

Sit back and picture this customer. Who are they really? Not just the school-like questions I listed above. Where do they get their hair done? What types of foods do they like to cook? Where do they shop? What would you buy for them Christmas if they were a friend? Get personal. Imagine an actual person. Heck, name them if you have to. You're a parent; you should be used to playing with imaginary friends by now!

***

REVIEWING PREVIOUS YEARS

Looking at the past years can be brutally hard but also brutally beneficial to the future of your business. Get old school and pull out a piece of paper, Excel or the ever-elusive sticky note. This will take time, but it will save you both time and money in the end. By examining the elements of cash flow (in and out) and marketing, the business goals can be adjusted for maximum return on investment.

First, write out each month of the year. Leave room for multiple columns. *You may want to work in pencil for this.* By dividing up incoming and outgoing cash flow based on the calendar month, you are readily able to identify the impact of outside influences such as marketing campaigns, holidays, and the introduction of new products.

Second, make columns for your business profit (products, services, referral fees etc.) and your cost of doing business (CODB). (See the business planning section above.)

This list does not include all of the expenses to be included in the cost of doing business. Keep in mind the expenses that you must pay in order to keep your business running.

Third, ensure all customer orders, sales tax, costs and profits are up to date. If you are a high volume business, it might be best to do these on a separate page and just carry over the totals. Now grab a second sheet of paper and write out the following:

- To Do

- To Improve

- To Eliminate

Fourth, evaluate the marketing investment cost (time and money) and the return on investment. These investments include your time spent, money spent and the money received. During which months was there a higher cash flow? If the marketing gave a high return on investment, place it in the "To Do" list. If it was lacking but saw a good response, add it to the

"To Improve" list. See where we are going with this? If it was more investment than you got back then put it in the "To Eliminate" list. Most simply, evaluate when the highest income months were and what action lead to the increased income.

Lastly, take the information you've pulled out and evaluate the costs of your business. Now is the time to plug leaks of money. Leaks in cash flow are lost profits. Don't want to do all this hard work? Consider this the next time you want to go on that Disney vacation or sign Little Timmy up for another sport but don't have the cash to do it. Plugging in some areas in which the return on investment is low will lead to increased profits.

See the end of the book for a business plan example

CHAPTER THREE:

WORKSPACE

Since you're reading this book you're probably a mom....and you're thinking, "Space? What space? You mean I get my own space?" Yes, and you need to demand it. This is a crucial aspect of running your business. It is driven by efficiency, productivity and industry. The stage and type of business will demand whether you are able to work from home or have to secure an out-of-home space. Other influencing factors to consider may include price, location, child-friendliness, insurance requirements, etc. It is important to list all of these out and consider them when determining which type of workspace is ideal for you as the business owner and most conducive to the bottom line. Besides, if you don't write it down, you know you won't remember it after running Timmy to soccer or making Sally's ballet tutu.

***

OUT-OF-HOME WORKSPACE

If your business demands, or you value your sanity, having an out-of-home workspace is great. But you must be realistic. When you hit the pavement and start looking at spaces or hit up design sites online, your imagination can run wild with all the great decorating ideas and the possibility of entertaining your customers. You may even slip into a daydream about how you might actually get to go to the bathroom without someone banging on the door or sliding Barbie shoes underneath it. Key things to keep in mind for an out-of-home space include overhead costs, functionality, close distance to home/children's activities and required insurance.

Pushing the curtain colors and carpet textures out of your head for a minute, let's get to thinking about how much it will cost you. Your cost of doing business figure (remember from Chapter 1?) should be listed out and ready for insertion of numbers. Jumping into a rental space out of mere survival instincts (think back to the Barbie shoe under the bathroom door ordeal) can end in disastrous results for the financial security and physical health of your business. Costs to think through when evaluating the workspace include mortgage/rent, furniture, utilities, insurance, technology install and maintenance.

A few things to consider include:

- Was the office space even in your business plan?
- Does it practically fit into your financial situation and goals?
- Are there budget cuts you can implement to make this work?
- Will this extend your goal timelines or reduce them?
- What can you do to make up the monetary investment?
- Will this truly benefit the business?

Evaluate these questions. Now that you've thought about them, get out your research document and make a new section for this! Write it down. Write everything down. Your goals and desires for a space may change by the time you get down to the nitty-gritty of having an out-of-home workspace. Always keep your eyes on what you want and the changes you've made to these desires.

The second most important aspect is that of functionality. If you haven't found a space, then list out the functional requirements you need. Note that I said need...not want. Just like anything else in life, there are things we must have and things that we would like to have. Finding an office space is no different.

Office space needs:

- Bathroom
- Electricity
- Office specific temperature controls
- Internet Connectivity
- Locked building, or front desk clerk
- Storage

Office space desires:

- More space than needed immediately
- Large windows
- Kitchen area
- Separate desk area from customer meeting area
- Cleaning staff

Laundry Tip: Industries are going to vary, so every business owner should be responsible and budget and prioritize according to specific needs.

A third important aspect of an out-of-home workspace is the proximity of the office to the home and/or children's activities. The balancing of family and business is knocked off kilter when a commute impedes upon a scheduled time. If you happen to live in a metropolitan area with public transit, the commute may not have a large impact as you can work via phone/tablet with wireless Internet. Then again, as a mom you may just want to use the commute to sneak in a nap. That in and of itself may be worth it! But as a whole, an office a reasonable distance away from the home will allow for easier scheduling, less stress rushing to or from work, and easy exits to activities and functions. (See the chapter on Scheduling and Maintaining Work Hours). Also, having a closer office location allows for popping in for shorter days when schedules get hectic. If the office is far away, this is nearly impossible and may force a home-office situation.

However, you should not choose a location based solely on proximity; rather, balance the distance from home with the actual location where the space is situated. Depending upon the industry, you may need to be prominently visible in the community to get customers in your doors. Also, the type of office will make a difference. If your industry is focused on a store or servicing customers, location and presentation will be important. If your business is web-based, the office may merely be a haven (read: oasis) to escape to in order to fulfill business responsibilities…and to sneak in that ever-elusive nap.

A fourth aspect of being a mom and running a business is that you may need an office space that will allow for children. If you entertain customers this may not be ideal, but having the option to allow your children to visit the office when they have a day off and you don't is an important aspect to balancing your business and your family.

Laundry Tip: Schedule appropriately so you don't have to take the kids into work, but allow for the fact that you can never fully predict what life will throw at you.

Life happens, and as business owners we must always be prepared. If your entire work is at this space, sometimes being able to run in with a sick kid on your hip to snag a few files might be a real benefit. It's easier to do this in a kid-friendly office without suitemates giving you the evil eye.

Laundry Tip: Always try to have the office and children's school or daycare within close proximity for ease of access.

The final aspect is that of access. Does the building allow you to control access at any time of the day? Being a working mom demands a flexible schedule and may require some late evenings at the office. Being bound to the timetable of a building that only allows for access during certain hours will infringe upon productivity and place extra pressure on you to force yourself to give on family time to fit into this schedule.

Laundry Tip: Never skimp on security or functionality in the name of saving money. If those aspects are the ones that have to give in order to afford a space then seek an alternative.

If you've found a space based on the above factors that you feel would work best for your situation but the money doesn't seem to be practical, consider sharing the space. Other local small business owners (and moms) may be seeking space out of the home for a way to separate their work life from home life as well. Get networked with other small business owners through trade organizations, Internet and community groups.

Additionally, if the money isn't adding up for the advertised price, contact the owner directly. The owner of the building may be flexible depending on the circumstances. Don't go in seeking an unreasonable bargain (as you wouldn't want that done to your product or services), but merely inquire as to what options may be available.

***

IN-HOME WORKSPACE

If you are newer in your business or merely enjoy hearing the kids trash the house while you attempt to answer a few emails, then an in-home office is the way to go. Kidding on the kids...sort of. Opting for an office in-home comes with rules and requirements, benefits and detriments to you, your business and your family.

Rules and Requirements

The very first rule of having an in-home workspace is to find a place that is away from the children, their toys and anything not directly related to your business. Being surrounded by the children, or even having them in view, will increase your anxiety and leave your mind distracted, as you have a constant reminder of any other things that need to be done.

An added bonus is thrown in if you're able to close off your area to keep little hands and wandering feet out of this work-only zone. Having defined house rules that separate the workspace from the living space helps to also define roles mentally and physically between mom and business owner. Sometimes the tiny psychological aspects of being in and around laundry or sharing space with other family members can diminish the productivity and successfulness of your small business. Besides that, little hands can occasionally get into files and cause mayhem.

> *When I was in law school, I had written this 30+ page brief, and walked away from my desk for all of two minutes to check on the laundry. I came back to find that my then 4 year old had edited and saved over the file. It*

was completely destroyed and I had to start almost at the beginning.

You're probably thinking, "Why didn't you have an additional copy?!" I learned after that to have one! (See the Organizational Chapter). I essentially lost three weeks worth of my brief, my thought process…and my sanity in two minutes. It was not worth it. While this was only lost time, it could have been lost money if it had happened to something related to business.

Laundry Tip: Always keep in mind the need for a separate and secluded space, especially away from prying eyes and pawing hands.

Benefits

Ahh. Now that we are past the requirements and boundaries of having a home office, let's chitchat about the benefits. Despite the horror story I just threw at you, there are great benefits to working from home. The first one is pretty obvious: unless you're on a videoconference the dress code is….whatever you want it to be! I have been known to get dressed to take kids to school, then come home and slip on yoga pants and slippers. There is absolutely nothing wrong with dressing down.

As a busy working mother, sometimes dealing with your appearance and dressing up can be a stressful and cumbersome task. While this is a benefit, it can also be a detriment as constant seclusion in the house with unwashed hair and wrinkled pajamas may lead to a downturn in your mental state. I do suggest embracing the benefit of no dress code, but also make sure you hop in the shower or run a brush through that bird's nest once in a while.

Working from home can be heaven when sickness strikes. It is perfect for the times your kids come home with pink eye it leaves so swollen you look like you had a run in with a mad plastic surgeon.

Not that I've ever been there....

Laundry Tip: Get up and get dressed as though you have to go out and face the public. Remain comfortable, but also maintain enough of an appearance so you feel like a productive member of society.

The second most obvious benefit is the lack of overhead and business functions that come with a rented/owned space. It is extremely nice to not have to worry about including this cost into the cost of doing business, as well as being exempt from contractual obligations and negotiations with landlord and ensuring business insurance is up to date.

I personally have opted to work from home while having children under the age of two, but this has led to wrangling children with the mute button on while trying to make sure the customer knows I am still engaged with what they are saying.

One time I inadvertently answered a phone call with the children home. I was absolutely unable to get off the phone to call the client back later (mostly for fear of losing the large contract deal). Well..my two-year-old was home causing a huge ruckus as she ran around clomping plastic princess shoes on our tile floor. I ran up the stairs and hid in the bathtub. Here I am crouched in a bathtub still damp from the morning shower and trying to talk to the client without giving away my secret hiding place. My goal was to hide from the screeching of "juuuusseee" so that I could close this deal. And of course, as you know, once a mother enters a bathroom every kid thinks it is time they need something or just want to chat. I peek out over the edge as little feet walked past me looking for me. End of story, I closed the deal and Princess Olivia had settled on the bathroom floor with my brush and her doll, none the wiser of my location.

Working moms gotta do - what they gotta do.

No matter the office space of choice, it is important to guarantee the environment is comfortably situated and sufficiently lit to reduce injury to eyesight and guarantee safety. If you select an out-of-home workspace, it is best to also have a dedicated area at home to allow for flexibility and focus. The danger of having a workspace in home is that many small business owners feel like they never leave work...or the house...or get to take a shower. The life of a working mom, right?

***

A HAPPY MEDIUM

Sometimes you absolutely cannot afford an out-of-home workspace, nor can you handle listening to Barney sing one more time while you try to do monthly accounting. This is where places with free wireless Internet come in handy. Finding a local coffee shop or restaurant that allows for you to use their Internet will permit for an escape, some human interaction (other than your little humans at home) and a few hours of productivity. The downfall of being in a public place is the tendency for the rate of effective productivity to drop depending on the type of worker you are. Some individuals can work and shut out the entire world. Others are unable to finish an email without watching the barista make the fourth Caramel Latte in the last half hour. It happens. Recognize what type you are. And sometimes, you just have to survive and hit up the local coffee shop even if you don't want to. Chances are your productivity level will be higher there than swimming in Legos and laundry at home.

In Home Office		Out of Home Office	
Pros	*Cons*	*Pros*	*Cons*
No rent	Lack of space	Tax Deduction	Overhead Increase
Can work sporadically	No place to meet customers	Separate Space	More insurance
More time with kids	Always surrounded by home obligations	Allows completely detachment from work, quantity over quality	Less time with kids
Child friendly	Distractions	More productive work time	Not always child friendly

***

WORKING TOWARDS A NEW OFFICE

Many mothers and small business owners opt for in-home office spaces for many of the positives and negatives outlined; some just don't want the overwhelming and frightening aspect of committing to an out-of-home workspace. However, a large number of small business owners find that working from home impedes their productivity and they begin to crave an external workspace or a more professional environment. Out-of-home workspace businesses find they outgrow the space or their demands/need change as the business progresses. All of these are reasons to keep a potential move to a new office on the periphery of your business plan.

Just like when you were beginning to determine what type of workspace you wanted initially, you must evaluate your business needs and a fiscal budget for making the move from an in-home to an out-of-home space. Reevaluate the business plan and budget to include a percentage earmarked for savings for an out-of-home workspace.

Laundry Tip: It can be exciting to start buying furniture and equipment ahead of time but wait until you know the actual size, space and aesthetics of your future space.

Perhaps a smart alternative in the interim would be to seek out communal offices or executive suites owned by other small business owners who are seeking to rent out space to achieve their own out-of-home workspace goals. These offices may even include their office equipment and supplies as part of the rental agreement, which reduces your overhead costs as well because you'll only be using what you need. This reduction in overhead costs can be carried over into the earmark for office savings to help move up your goal timeline.

Keep in mind the factors mentioned previously about location, commute time, and property amenities. Factor all these into a budget to make that move out of the corner of the "Lego meets Batman Kingdom" playroom and into a professional (and quiet) workspace.

***

OFFICE SUPPLIES

No matter what type of office space you end up going with, you will need office supplies. These will often vary dependent upon industry and your affinity for post-it notes or colored highlighters. Office supplies are a lot like office space amenities: there are needs and there are wants. There is definitely a market full of various gizmos and gadgets but this is another area to plug a leak of money that has little return. Office supplies are stuck in the overhead category as they are used to run your business; they are not an investment that you directly receive a return on. You should try to limit them as much as possible. Besides, you don't really want to have to choose between new little tot soccer league pictures or fancy paperclips, do you? Didn't think so.

Needs:
- Paper
- Pens, Pencils, Highlighters
- Filing Organization Supplies
- Calendars, Planners
- Electronics (Computers, printers, smart phone)
- Office maintenance supplies (light bulbs, trash bags)
- Furniture (desk and chair)
- Back up data system

Wants:
- Post it notes
- High quality legal pads
- Automatic stapler
- Expensive electronics that offer more than what your business requires

Laundry Tip: Look at ordering in bulk to keep costs per unit low.

Some office products can be eliminated when everything is digital, but keep in mind the need for a data backup system or two. Calendars, planners, to do lists and files can all be done digitally and stored on external hard drives or in a cloud. I prefer this method over hard files simply because if you are stuck at home with a sick kid, there is no need to run to grab files. You can just boot up the computer and snag them out of the cloud! So look into the option of keeping your files in digital storage if that is a realistic plan for your business.

Notice that I put smart phone under need. Customers have no idea and often disregard that you have a home life and other obligations. Being able to work on the go through mobile devices (phones or tablets) will allow for quick crossing off of to-do list items throughout the day without requiring you to be tethered to your desk.

As a mother running two businesses, I need a smart phone with Internet. It is a must. You are probably thinking, "Okay, this girl is whacko." Stick with me. You'll see throughout the book how important it is to be as flexible as possible and work wherever you are. Yes, even in the emergency room at midnight, with a two-year old passed out on you after having just thrown up curdled milk. And you have no change of clothes. Sometimes you do what you have to do. You'd be surprised what you can get done when it's sink or swim. Not that I've done that...not me.

***

No matter where or how you choose to work, all that matters if that you get stuff done. There's no right or wrong way to do it. Everyone's personality, family structure, resources and qualifications are going to result in varying business models and approaches to getting things accomplished. Choose a workspace that works for you and, like everything else, reevaluate periodically to see if it is impeding on your productivity and profits in a negative or positive manner.

CHAPTER FOUR:

GETTING TASKS DONE

This chapter would seriously be the easiest one to explain if I could just say, "OUTSOURCE!" But alas, not all of us can afford to outsource, or may not even want to for certain aspects of the business. There are even some tasks we simply cannot push off on an intern or hired help.

So to combat being buried under cumbersome tasks, we must institute measures to get tasks done. These include setting hours, calendar scheduling, to-do lists, automation, wrap ups/reviews, and figuring out how to balance household obligations amongst it all.

While you may have been in business for a long time, or a short time, schedules, to-do lists and workflow charts are never obsolete.

At about a year into my consulting business I knew my exact workflow, and had my finger on the pulse of my clients. I drifted away from this running to-do list and relied on myself to remember it all. Then one-night I sat up in bed, cold sweats and realized that I had forgotten to follow up with a big contract. Potential networking. Potential for large amount of money. Potential for more exposure. I flew down the stairs, attempting to not kill myself, and started banging out a follow up email to the contact. It had only been a couple days longer than if I had scheduled my follow-up email but still..in my heart I knew that every day that passed was potential for a lost contract. Right then and there I spent a couple hours pouring everything onto paper and into my digital calendar.

Do I still miss the personal deadline for follow-ups sometimes? Sure. I'm human. But my customer experience has become consistent and much more efficient across the board. My schedule has defined my personal and customer expectations. And as a result I'm a much more organized and happier business owner (AND MOM!)

***

SETTING A SCHEDULE OR NOT

The first most important piece of advice I can give you is to make set hours. The very next advice is to throw it out the window...for the most part. This section should probably be more appropriately titled "Not Committing to a Schedule." Like most things with being a mother, you should always expect to be flexible. But don't be Gumby. You don't want to be so flexible that the business hours start to overtake the family hours; because it is a slippery slope once you're there.

Stick to a certain amount of hours per week. This will help your sanity, recordkeeping and income level. By paying yourself a steady salary based on hours worked, consistency will unfold. But with these certain amount of hours comes flexibility.

For example, say Little Timmy has a preschool play at 10am one day but you typically try to work 8-5. So what?! Unless you have a pressing deadline or customer product/service to deliver, be flexible. Take yourself down there with your camera in hand to capture every minute of the play.

Laundry Tip: Guess what? You're the BOSS! Don't forget it! Run your business, don't let it run you.

Yes, you just might need to make that time up, but who better to approve this mid-day absence than the boss (ahem...that's you)? Tack on an extra hour elsewhere in the day or week. When the anxiety of stepping out mid-work day (whatever your hours may be) starts to rise, just think about why you became a business owner in the first place. More than likely one of the reasons was so that you could be in charge. But are you really in charge if you're letting the business run you? As always, keep a balance, making sure you are getting your work done but not to the detriment of your family and yourself.

***

IDENTIFYING CUSTOMER EXPECTATIONS

Identifying customer expectations will help to formulate the next few parts that we are going to go over (prioritizing tasks, scheduling and all that jazz). Knowing what your customers expect and what you want to deliver will help to provide a foundation on which you can build your plan to get tasks done. It is extremely important to note that there are reasonable and unreasonable expectations from customers. In this day and age with the onslaught of social media and technology, expectations can be skewed, as the public is demanding an "on demand" response or delivery of product despite physical, business or legal constraints. The reason this is of such importance is that chasing down unreasonable expectations is a waste of time, money, and emotional investment.

The more time spent on actions with little return on investment is essentially like the time my son took my Blackberry PDA/phone and threw it out the window as we were driving down the highway. Do what?

Oh yes....I was driving down the highway with the windows down, wind in our hair and music turned up to sing along. I glance in the rearview mirror to see my work issued Blackberry (employment prior to entering self-employment) skipping down the highway. Apparently he got bored playing brick breaker and didn't know of another way to dispose of said electronic system.

Oh yeah...imagine me explaining that one to the boss.

Any action that is attempting to appease and feed unreasonable expectations of unreasonable customers results in a loss for your business and yourself. Imagine how the Blackberry looked after that trip down Interstate 95 outside Washington D.C. That is exactly how you're going to end up feeling after continually appeasing your unrealistic customers. This beat-up feeling will unfortunately enter into your psyche and manifest as frustration, exhaustion and demotivation. All of these will creep into other areas of the business and your home life, which do absolutely no one any good. The last thing we want is Little Timmy asking you to cut out paper snowflakes with him, only to be told no because the exhaustion from continually trying to chase these unreasonable expectations. Those expectations should never become a barrier to enjoying those little moments with your children.

Reasonable Expectations

- Timely response to communications (48-72 hours).

- Providing enough information through the website, brochure or storefront to relay types of products/services, descriptions, and starting prices.

- Issuing of refunds or product delivery within quoted policy timelines.

Unreasonable Expectations

- Immediate response to communications (less than 24 hours and outside office hours).

- Refunds to be issued for circumstances not covered in your policy or due to the customer's fault. Example: Customer purchases a digital product but fails to comply with internet/computer requirements and demands a refund despite having been informed in the product description.

- Customer expecting you to meet deadlines without contracted responsibilities fulfilled on customer's side of the agreement. Example: An accountant not receiving all requested financial forms by deadline unable to fulfill obligation of creating and delivering fiscal report.

- Expecting the business to be open on company set holidays.

Questions to ask to identify customer expectations

- Do my customers expect an immediate response?

- Am I able to set up supports in place to provide customers information or an experience with my company before I am able to get back to them (website, etc.)?

- Are my employees, if any, equipped to handle business in my absence? If not, what can I do to prepare them?

- Will not having standard hours hurt my customer relationships? (Remember that every business needs structure and not to let customers unreasonably dictate your business)

Keep in mind, what might be an unreasonable expectation under a certain set of circumstances may convert to a reasonable expectation depending on the industry, job and deadlines approaching.

Laundry Tip: Always consider each situation and the development of policies with an open mind and thoughtful process of consequences that may require damage control for yourself (exhaustion) or your business (bad publicity).

***

TO-DO LISTS AND PRIORITIZING TASKS

In order to be productive in the flexible hours that you do reserve for yourself, it is extremely effective to have a running to-do list and prioritized order for action. Having both of these on hand and readily accessible will allow for quick entry into the important tasks at hand so you can maximize the productivity in the hours that you do work. This also helps to create a consistent experience across the board that customers can come to expect and rely on during their business relationship with you.

By having to spend a decent chunk of time each morning figuring out what to do for the day, you are spending less time on important tasks or wasting time that could be put toward your family time. Have to-do lists and workflow steps prominently displayed or accessible for use.

Ways to Display To-Do Lists:

- Custom Whiteboard

     Have a custom made whiteboard with a checklist of customer workflow steps

- Plain whiteboard

     For smaller daily to-do lists have a blank white board that is easily reached

- Large Calendar

     Keep a large calendar on the wall for easy reference

- Running Digital List

     Keep a running digital list in a word processing document, spreadsheet or application

A running to-do list can be organized into two main categories: over-arching (global) tasks and immediate tasks.

Over-arching tasks include all items that are in need of being worked on or accomplished in the foreseeable future. The immediate tasks include those with approaching deadlines and daily routine activities.

Laundry Tip: Your daily and over-arching (global) tasks can change up as the business demands. Be flexible.

Example of Running To-Do List

Daily	Over-arching
Customer Inquiries	Update Website
Social Media Engagement	Filing of customer documents
	Re-ordering office supplies

A structural framework for a running to-do list of daily priorities for businesses will look similar to this. *Note: Will vary dependent upon industry.*

- Top Priority - Responses to inquiries, orders, social media engagement and customer service communications

- Medium Priority - Business related transactions such as marketing inquiries, potential business opportunities, day-to-day overhead responsibilities

- Low Priority - Email responses to non-crucial players should come as time permits. These include inquiries from local organizations, schools, etc.

For example, an individual with a consulting or service based business would have the following running to-do list.

- Top Priority – Responding to customer inquiries, following up with previous inquiries, customer product orders and populating Internet sites with upcoming session specials

- Medium Priority – Responding to or sending out inquiries for business relationships with local photographers, vendors and small businesses as marketing opportunities, designing and ordering marketing materials for upcoming events

- Low Priority – Revamping product packaging and researching new products

Laundry Tip: Don't be shy to include family daily to-dos. If they are important and need to be accomplished they are every bit as important as the business to-dos.

This to-do list should also be accompanied by deadlines on the calendar and written in a priority order.

***

WORKFLOW AND CALENDAR

As soon as a commitment is made, whether formal (product delivery date) or informal (promising to follow up with a customer), put it on the calendar. Consider including "Calendar Submission" as part of your customer workflow. No matter the industry you will find that you take the same workflow procedures to see a customer through from beginning to end. Whether it is a photography customer that you see through the shooting process, or a salon customer you want to convert into repeat business, there are methodical steps.

Business owning = busy = distracted

Being working mom = even the kids are lucky some days to get their hair brushed. See my point?

Unless you have successfully outsourced this area (see the chapter on outsourcing), the responsibility to remember everything rests on your shoulders. Having set workflow procedures that include this calendar submission will increase the probability of following through and increasing the customer experience. Basically: If you find yourself doing it repeatedly, quit running into a wall and institute it as a normal step in your workflow through automation or templates. If you keep banging your head into a wall, it doesn't hurt less. It is counterproductive.

Laundry Tip: Taking time to front-load by identifying workflow steps and instituting measures to make the workflow more efficient will save more time in the end.

The trick to a successful calendar is ease of access to the schedule and identifying priority tasks through identifying marks. Ease of access to the calendar may be accomplished through the use of a smart phone, tablet, or computer with wireless Internet connectivity, or even by going old school with a day planner. Having a calendar on hand will allow for quick adjustments in daily workflow, enabling you to make the spontaneous decision to skip out for a surprise lunch at your child's elementary school cafeteria. Identifying marks and color-coded entries can also help you make quick adjustments in daily plans. Just like with the email color-coding, using a standard system to identify high priority and low priority will increase efficiency in daily decision making and accomplishing tasks.

***

AUTOMATE, AUTOMATE!

Sometimes we just have to automate, and sometimes it is better that we do! Automation can lend to more efficiency as we have less jumbling our mom brains because the tasks are being accomplished without thought on our part. Automation can lend to efficient prioritizing of tasks such as email labeling, newsletter messaging systems, social media posting systems and calendar scheduling.

In most industries, emails are the center point of communications, and on some days they can be the bane of our existence. Especially Monday mornings....can I get an amen to that one, sister? I sometimes dread Mondays because of the amount of emails that will be sitting there waiting for me. You know, if I actually allowed myself to not work during the weekend that is! Email labeling or tagging is a crucial aspect of helping prioritize daily tasks. This can help turn your mountain of emails into small little hills you can conquer one at a time.

I totally admit to having a quick flash to Braveheart-style charging up a hill...but I digress.

The email you use will depend on how the emails are categorized, but the idea is that keywords or addresses are set up to be labeled in certain categories. To take the organization a step further, set up various folders to direct these labeled emails. This will allow you to run through your daily to-do list in priority order without having to open each email and decide which to answer first.

Examples:

- Website submissions through a contact form always come from the same email address. Tag this email address to go to an Inquiry folder.

- Constant contact with one person is a marketing opportunity. Tag this email to be diverted to the Marketing folder.

After labeling and directing emails to the appropriate folder, you can take it a step further (again, depending on email customer) and dedicate a specific color to each task to allow for quick priority recognition at a glance.

Examples:

- Product orders through your website may be color-coded as red for high-priority attention.
- Follow ups from local businesses or organizations inquiring as to a future get-together event may be color-coded as yellow or green for medium to low priority attention depending upon the calendar and marketing plan schedule.

***

WRAP UPS AND REVIEWS

Having all these ideas in place means absolutely nothing if the tasks aren't being accomplished. Institute into your schedule a wrap-up and review process of a set time schedule. This is especially important when it comes to taxes. I just heard a groan come from deep within you, but I promise by instituting a wrap up of taxes you will thank me.

Think about it this way: You keep everything filed and organized, but don't load it into your spreadsheets or expense tracking program, figuring that your organized files will save you at the end of the year. Wrong. The timing of this is horrible. As time creeps into December, the stress and hustle of the holidays increases. By the end of the year business owners are pretty much ready to shelve things until 2013.

Okay...that doesn't sound so bad...
...I'll push it off until January.

Oh, really?

Then what about all the beginning of the year tasks that need done (i.e. marketing campaigns, customer services, production of new items, etc.)? You will then be forced to hole up in your office for a day, or two...or three going through all of your folders and information to input everything. (Side note: This is one area I really recommend outsourcing if possible). End result? Taking time away from kicking off the New Year fresh and never catching up without great detriment to yourself and your schedule. You know those nights the kids never sleep and you feel like you're never going to catch up? Take that feeling and add on the IRS deadline. Kind of didn't think you wanted to go there!

So the tax example seems extreme, but it's not. Not that I've *ever* done that. No. Not me. Never. HA! But realistically, you should always be on top of organization and accounting. If you're sitting there and thinking that you've got that down, let's look at your reviewing of your business and marketing plans. Are you committing honest evaluations and critiques of business actions and marketing campaigns? Waiting until an entire year, or even half of a year, has passed to evaluate these will leave you in your competitors' dust. And it will leave you exhausted, much like rocking faster in a rocking chair but going absolutely nowhere. Or trying to clean the house with two toddlers and a dog running around spilling mac and cheese on everything. Ahh...now you get it!

***

BALANCING HOUSEHOLD OBLIGATIONS

Working In-Home

One may think that working in-home means you have plenty of time for chores. Wrong. I have found from working both sides of the coin that working in-home can be harder. It is easy to get sucked into the idea that you need to have everything done at once.

Remember our to-do lists?

Those little buggers are just as important for the household duties. Having these running to-do lists will allow for proper allocation of time and will avoid embarrassment when you show up at Sally's ballet bake sale sans cupcakes.

Working Out of Home

Just like running your business needs organization, so does your home. I'm going to adopt the same methods two-year-olds do to bang something into your head. Going to repeat myself…again.

Schedule, schedule, schedule.

Put everything into the calendar. By scheduling all aspects, the entire family will know what is going on at all times, which sets expectations for fulfillment of obligations. The schedule also provides boundaries for priorities.

***

HOW AM I GOING TO MAKE THIS HAPPEN FO REAL?

Now go write everything down in your business plan. Oh yes, we are even planning hours. You are more likely to commit to your plan if it is in writing. Even if you never look at it again, hopefully it will be a telltale heart, beating to remind you that family comes first. Here are a few questions to help you formulate this part of your plan.

- What is your plan for your hours worked?

- What is your flexible schedule going to look like?

- Are you just going to work until everything is done?

- What about priorities? How much are you really being compensated for your time?

- What automation techniques can you implement?

- Does your current email customer offer filtering and color-coding? If not, should you move to a new platform while retaining the address?

- What can I do to better manage customer expectations?

- Am I relaying my expectations of my customers appropriately?

- Am I providing customers enough information to understand my policies?

Let's take it a step further. Not only are you going to outline the hours and flexibility guidelines, but you are also going to write out the customer workflow procedures mentioned above. Write a manual as though you are handing over your entire office to someone else to run for a week. Who knows? You might just need a quick flight to Hawaii for a Mai Tai on the beach sans kids!

MARKETING PREFACE

Like everything else so far discussed we must be as efficient as possible. Marketing is an area that is an on-going contact sport. Without marketing a business will stall and fall flat on its face. Kinda like you did when you stepped on a bazillion Legos in the dark trying to get to the coffee pot. Just like that.

It may not take as much skill as navigating the landmine of Legos or Barbie shoes but it is a constant battle that must be fought. The great thing about marketing is that the more effort put in at the beginning and to keep evaluating return on investment (for what is working and is not) helps to keep the marketing rolling along. There are two primary avenues to marketing, online and offline. Cultivating both platforms for marketing will help propel the business forward and keep marketing effectively by instituting efficiency measures.

CHAPTER FIVE:

MARKETING ONLINE

In this day and age, any business would be foolish to ignore social media and online presences. This is especially true for working parents. Unlike other traditional marketing aspects, social media and online campaigns can be started, ended and evaluated on a whim. These actions may also be the most cost effective marketing techniques, as many social media accounts are free to advertise on and reach audiences. Working parents should capitalize on prices because, with the onslaught of online marketing, more companies are driven to competitive pricing for similar products or services.

Before we go any further I just want to say:

YOUR ONLINE PRESENCE WILL SAVE YOU TIME

YOUR ONLINE PRESENCE WILL MAKE YOU MONEY.

IT WILL MAKE YOU TIME AND MONEY.

By recognizing the aspects of each, spending time to set up and routinely maintain an online presence the marketing ball keeps on rolling for your business and frees up time that would have otherwise been spent elsewhere. And who doesn't need a few more hours in the day to hand tie-dye all of Little Timmy's soccer league shirts?

***

CREATE A WEBSITE

Obviously the first step is to get yourself online. Creating a website can be extremely overwhelming. The most important thing is to breathe. Sit back in your office chair, hands behind your head, and close your eyes. Think about 3-5 things you want your website to do for you and how you want to it talk about you. Anything that you can implement into your marketing strategy that markets FOR you is well worth investing time and money into. Here are some tips to think about when creating your website (or when hiring someone else to create it):

Tips for Creating a Website

- Is it easy to edit and update with fresh content?

Laundry Tip: If a website is too difficult to edit or update with fresh content, you won't do it. Find a website that always allows for simple insertion of information.

- Does it represent my brand?

- Are you getting enough return on the financial and time investment on the website?

- Is it user-friendly for clients?

- Does it convey what business I am in?

Websites do not necessarily need tons of bells and whistles, but should look professional, provide pertinent information to customers and have the capability to become a hub for your business. While being user friendly is important, your website should also provide enough information that can be understood even by a 3am web-surfing mom who is scared to move from the rocking chair for fear of waking a teething baby.

Laundry Tip: Your goal is to keep your viewers engaged and interested in business and not frustrated by vagueness.

***

CREATE A BLOG

Blogging is a front running way for businesses to become known on the web. Social media, as you will see, is widespread but is not the "home" in which your business lives, breathes and does laundry. Blogs also give your business a face and a voice that social media does not provide. Imagine this: social media platforms are simply shouts at a stranger on the street. A blog is pulling that stranger into your home and letting them get to know you.

Tips to Blogging Effectively:

- Look professional

    Find a blog platform that is easily editable and customizable to your brand but also looks professional. It is a bonus if this integrates with your website.

- Use Google analytics

    Google analytics is a no-brainer! This service allows a code to be embedded in your site, and then does market research for you. Forget having to pound the pavement or send out surveys all the time. Identify demographics and locations of your audience, as well as how long they are on your site, how many pages are visited, which posts are viewed the most and a whole bunch of information that would have taken enough time to collect that it will rival the length of time that you've been dreaming of a day off!

- Encourage your readers to share

  Place share buttons for the various social media platforms that are available. Giving your readers the tools to talk about you will mean more of an audience without you doing any work! Now if only the laundry worked the same way…

- Converse with your audience

  Don't present to them a board meeting or a rendition of your resume. Talk to them. They are people. Be the voice you are in your home. Not in the boardroom (and I'm not talking the "go to bed or I'm taking away your Barbie" voice).

- Don't be a billboard

  Quit talking about your products or services only. Pair products or services with related content that is interesting to read. Subtle marketing is the way to go.

We have the website, we have the blog, but now we have to make it work for you! Never underestimate the power and credibility a blog can give your business. During the second year of business I committed to blogging weekly. Every single Monday was dedicated to blogging. Not only was I seeing my audience grow but also the respect they had for me as an expert, as a wealth of knowledge.

***

KEY IN ON SEARCH ENGINE OPTIMIZATION

At the very core of an online presence for a website or blog is search engine optimization (SEO). This process affects the visibility and search-ability of a webpage or blog in various search engines. This process is a primary Internet marketing strategy that is continually built through various procedures. Through the use of key words, back links and repeated fresh content, a website is more likely to be visible to search engines, in turn, be more visible to customers seeking out products or services on the web.

In plain terms, it's like telling your kids to go pick up a specific toy. They enter their crazy messy rooms to find this item. By repeatedly telling them what item you're referring to you're more likely to receive that item back. If you take an extended break from reminding them what a certain item is called they are less likely to remember and unable to retrieve it. The search engine "crawlers" work in a similar fashion by sorting through the messy "rooms" of the Internet to retrieve the toy (your information). The end goal is to fine tune SEO for your site and to be as visible as possible to your customers as they search with certain keywords.

Tips to Search Engine Optimization:

- Have fresh content regularly

  Having a blog or an updated website will help to fine tune the crawlers. The web crawlers begin to get bored with old information, thus resulting in a slipping of visibility. Further, fresh content will drive audiences. Everyone wants to see what everyone else is seeing. These crawlers are no different.

- Use keywords

  Think about the key terms that clients would sit down to search for to find a company with products or services like you have. Use these keywords in blog SEO plugins, in the text of blog posts, and in website headers (to name a few).

- Name your pictures properly

  If you include images on your site, then consider naming them the same as the keywords mentioned above. Crawlers cannot view pictures but rather see the data behind them (including the name of the file). This will also allow for your website to be searchable under image searches, which maximizes the search channels available to potential customers.

- Get a domain keyword

  By having a domain that literally reads the key words you want people to use to find you will aid in SEO. Example:

  Keywords Wanted: Photography Business Consulting

Domain:
http://www.photographybusinessconsulting.com

- Longevity

  The longer you are around, the more credible and visible your site becomes. Pair this with fresh content and audiences for maximum results.

Laundry Tip: Search engines and their functions will change over time; therefore, some of these functions may vary in their effectiveness. Always check out tutorials to save yourself wasted time.

So you're probably thinking, "How am I even going to touch on all this and still have time to make dinner?" Stick with me. These steps can be instituted into your workflow every time you go to check on your site. Here are some quick ways to fine tune your website or blog to SEO:

- Blog regularly

  By having a blog with related information for your industry, the keywords will be spilling all over the place. This will also build up credibility for you as a primary or front running company on that type of product or service. Even blogging once or twice a month will key in optimization and add fresh content for your audience. Think you don't have time? Take out your handy-dandy smart phone and type out 5-10 tips about a topic pertinent to your business while you're waiting on the dishwasher to finish its cycle. Bam. Done!

- Check up on your site

Just like when you have a storefront, there should be routine checks on links, contact forms, accessibility of information, ease of navigability, and updated product or services information.

- Get others to talk about you

  Consider reaching out to other companies in your industry that have blogs and social media platforms to work with you on a partnership of promoting one another. This can be compensated through affiliate sales or a set advertising fee. If another company provides a content driven blog post paired with your company link, you will receive multiple benefits including a backlink, keyword optimizing and broader reach of audience.

- Encourage customers to share

  On your website or blog encourage your customers to share your product, service, and website or blog post. There are various plug-ins for the different social media platforms available depending upon your website or blog set up. A simple "call to action" for your customers to share will increase the exposure of your website as they are shared via social media.

- Be distinct

  Do something different. The things that go "viral" are those that are not the same. Think about how you can break outside the box, or take a mainstream idea and put YOUR spin on it. Be you.

***

USE SOCIAL MEDIA PLATFORMS

A second key to an online marketing strategy is through the use of social media sites. I know you're thinking, "There are so many!" Well good! I'm going to show you the trick to making it so you don't have to grease the wheels on all of them. Remember back to the marketing section where we discussed target market? Well, in order to bring that target customer in the door you must go to where they are.

Finding Your Target Customer on Social Media:

- What demographic characteristics does your target customer have?

- Which social media platforms have the most quality (or quantity)?

- What social media platforms is your target customer frequenting?

- At what level are they using it? Socializing? Seeking services or products?

- How often are your target customers on this social media platform?

Now that you know all that information, you need to maximize your efficiency in postings. To maximize efficiency in your social media you must post at critical times of day, even if you can't be at a computer, and use certain key words. Lost marketing ground on social media is gone forever. It is just as important, if not more, for social media to have fresh content and visibility like your website.

Using Social Media Effectively (General Tips)

- Keep all social media accounts branded

    Try to keep all account names relatively the same across the platforms. The key is to allow your company's name and presence to be easily recognizable, known and readily searchable.

- Post during prime times

    Crucial high audience traffic times can fluctuate depending on the target market but are typically mid-morning, mid-afternoon and evening. Obtaining a service that allows one publishing to push to all various social media sites will increase efficiency and cut down on wasted time.

- Schedule social media posts

    Many of these services have a scheduling function that allow for time-based publishing. This will allow for one-stop development of social media campaigns to be created then strategically published for maximized return (See scheduling posts).

- Engage your audience

    Each social media post should have a call to action – whether it is "share this picture" or asking a question in a status. The visibility of social media posts increases the amount of your audience that engages with it.

    Also get to know your audience. Start by engaging your audience you can get to know them on a personal level. One day I was surfing around Facebook and checking out profiles of my fans. Lo and behold two of my fans were individuals I had gone to elementary school with when we were stationed with the military overseas. These fans didn't know who I was because I was operating under my married name and not my maiden name. Not only was I noticing the reach of my social media but also I was able to reconnect and further my network by reaching out to these past friends.

- Use a picture

    Pair blog posts, sales or information with a picture. Pictures are quite often likely to show up in social media platform newsfeeds more prominently than merely words. They will also be more eye-catching and more likely to engage your audience.

- Place your contact info prominently

    What is the point in gaining viewers of your info if you aren't going to let them know how to contact you or obtain your product/service?

- Keep up with the terms of service

    Always keep up with the terms of service so that you do not violate the terms. Violation can result in removal of your account and lost networking with audience.

- Personalize your profile

    Let the audience have a description of who you are and what you do. Customers are quite often more attracted to a certain business when they know the face behind it.

Here is a basic rundown on the key aspects of using some prominent social media platforms currently beneficial for businesses.

Note: I said currently. Tides change so quickly with social media that one day these may be obsolete...which gets us into the discussion of not putting all your eggs in one basket that is to come later.

Each of these tips are quick action items that can be placed on your daily or weekly workflow list to gain online exposure.

#1 Twitter

Twitter is a social media platform that consists of prominently text-based updates known as "tweets". The key to using Twitter is that tweets are short and simple in that they only allow a maximum of 140 characters. These short tweets help to drive home marketing campaigns without all the fluff.

Twitter Tips:

- Tweet regularly

   This might seem like a given, but on Twitter you need to tweet. Even more so than you may need to post on other social media platforms. Also, because of the high-content nature of Twitter you are able to be a guide in educating your audience through re-tweeting and favoriting of other industry-related companies.

- Be short and sweet

Due to character restrictions, try to stay away from short hand but be mindful of the character limitation when crafting statuses. Also, consider using link shorteners to make your long website or blog link into a succinct short link.

- Use hashtags

  Use the hashtag sign (#) to identify and categorize your posts by topic. Use categories such as company name and industry. This is a two-second marketing method to reach a larger audience outside of your followers.

- Connect Twitter

  Twitter is one of the primary social platforms that works well being connected to others. Use it to push out information to various other platforms to expedite your marketing and increase exposure.

#2 Facebook

Facebook is another social media platform that allows for status updates, sharing of photos, sharing of links, and joining of community groups. A major benefit of Facebook is that the structure allows for users to have personalized profiles for friends and family but also to readily interact with business pages without requiring an acceptance.

Facebook Tips:

- Profile and timeline cover photos

Make sure your branding is consistent for your company through your profile and timeline cover photos. If you are a one-woman show, then show it! Show your face. Put a human face to the name of your business.

- Use photographs

  Facebook feeds can move quickly but are the perfect place to pair promotions, status updates, launch of new products/services and blog posts with a picture. Use graphics that are cohesive to branding and eye-catching.

- Network

  Get into groups with like industry businesses to gain exposure and network connections.

- Create a community group

  Depending on the product or service you provide, create a group to interact with your audience. Service based companies will greatly benefit from interaction with audiences. Keep in mind: this requires upkeep that may be too much for some schedules.

#3 Pinterest

Pinterest is a social media platform that does not allow status updates; rather, it works as a virtual pinboard to share photos that are linked to various web links. Users of Pinterest can follow various boards and repin (share) interesting links.

Pinterest Tips:

- Create your own pin board

  Create a board as a hub for your audience to find you on Pinterest. Gone are the days that Pinterest is solely for craft ideas and recipes. Many businesses are using boards to collectively and aesthetically show their products and services.

- Use a "Pin it" button

  Use a widget or plugin to prominently place a "Pin it" button on your website next to blog posts, products or contact information. Every time you publish new content, pin your own content to your own pin board.

#4 Instagram

Like Pinterest, Instagram is a photo sharing social media platform; however, it does not have pinboards. Rather, Instagram users can have followers and follow one another's photo feeds. The platform also allows for a variety of editing functions on pictures, captioning of photos and hashtag category identifiers.

Instagram Tips:

- Connect and publish

  Instagram is another primary social medium platform that has readily accessible publishing settings across other social media platforms.

- Showcase your products/services

    Seek out and take pictures of creative ways to display your products or services.

- Use captions

    Use the captions to write "calls of action" or promotions to your audience.

- Use hashtags

    Like with Twitter, use hashtags to draw attention to your posts by topic.

- Show behind the scenes

    Use this platform to show fun and exclusive behind the scenes actions of your business. If you're a lawyer, simply post a photograph of that day's courthouse with a fun filter. A writer could use this service to take behind the scenes shots of the writing process. This could serve as a tease to your audience regarding the products or services you have available to them, capturing their interest and encouraging them to do more research on your business.

#5 Google+

Google+ is a social media platform and networking site owned by the large site engine Google. This platform allows for viewings of newsfeeds called 'streams,' which are updates from various identified 'circles.' The circles are created by organizing other Google+ users. This platform is also the only current site that provides video group chats in 'hangouts'.

Google+ Tips:

- Use Google hang outs

  Set up webinars and hangouts to provide content-based presentations to your audience to sell products and/or services.

- Use Google events

  Use Google Events to send out customized invitations to your network, whether Google+ users or not, for events.

- Use Circles

  When your audience fans you, you can reciprocate by including them into "circles." This works as a great marketing tool as it compiles a "circle" for segmenting out the audience for target marketing.

#6 Linkedin

LinkedIn is a social media site for individuals in professional occupations intended to facilitate networking on a professional level. This platform works as a virtual business card holder, as contact networks are built and saved virtually. The site also allows users to upload their resume for potential employers to view and consider for employment. Functions of sharing photos and bookmarking allow for users to save the content they have viewed for future reference.

LinkedIn Tips:

- Start a community group

    Initiate and maintain a community group based on a topic that is directly relevant to your business or your audience.

- Browse the groups

    Open your eyes and see what the groups have to say. Free market research is at your fingertips! It may take some time to wade through it all but for those on a budget and wanting honest opinions, this is your place to find them.

#7 Youtube

YouTube is the only social media platform that is primarily a video-sharing website. Status updates, sharing of photos and links are nonexistent; however, in their place comes videos and advertisements. Many small businesses are using YouTube public sharing and "My Channel" functions to share information by video with their current audience and to reach new audience members.

YouTube Tips:

- Create content

    Well, obviously you need video content. Consider creating some key content videos to place on your website and onto your own dedicated YouTube Channel.

- Encourage subscribers

Encourage your audience to follow you on the channel so that they are given automated updates of your newly published content. Also, at the end of each video encourage them to share it.

- Use keywords

  Make your videos searchable with keywords that readily identify your company and product/service. Get into a routine of adding key words to your descriptions so that your videos come up during searches by audience and non-audience members.

***

NEWSLETTER SUBSCRIBERS

Remember how I mentioned not putting all of your eggs in one basket? Here is a way to make sure you have an extra basket for a rainy day. A crucial online marketing strategy is through newsletter lists pulled from contact submissions or opt-in forms. These customer lists, potential or existing, are gold. These are the fuel on which your marketing planning runs. Through the use of your website contact submission forms or strategically placed newsletter opt-in forms, you will have a plethora of customers at your fingertips.

Organically built newsletter lists have a tendency to work better because the individuals you are contacting wanted to be on your list at some point. They either wanted to be on it for an incentive, interest or future interest in your product or services. It is easier to cultivate an audience that is willing to listen than an audience that doesn't necessarily want to, which is what happens when you purchase newsletter list contacts.

It is similar to attempting to have your children do their chores. If there is something for them to get out of it, whether it is a toy or trip to the park, they are more likely to listen and are amenable to what you have to say. If they are vehemently against leaving the house or just simply in a bad mood, they will not listen and will shut you down. The shutting down aspect may not necessarily be a bad thing, as you are then closing off an ineffective marketing channel resulting in saved time, money and investment. So what should you do? Build your list. Be strategic.

Keys to Building and Maintaining a Newsletter List:

- Incentivize it

  Offer an incentive for customers to sign up (Example: Coupon code for a percentage off of first order).

- Follow up

  Follow up with inquiries and place them on this list. Just because one person happened to not take part in your service or product immediately does not necessarily mean they won't be interested later. Give them a personalized customer experience.

- Strategic placement

  Strategically place newsletter opt-in forms on your site (Examples: at check out, within a blog post, or on the front page).

- Segment your list

Target your marketing efforts on key segments of your newsletter list. Targeting can occur based on the previous spending trends of the individuals, demographics, location, etc.

- Automated Market Research

    Choose a newsletter service that generates reports with data including open rates, spam filters, commerce conversions, and location. This allows your newsletter (and voluntary subscriber) to do the work of market research for you.

All in all social marketing is a godsend for parents. It provides an optimal platform for marketing on the go and reaching the most amount of people. You can continue marketing campaigns whether from the sidelines of Timmy's soccer practice or soaking in a tub. Although I highly recommend separating family and business time, the option *is* always there to stay connected if need be.

CHAPTER SIX:

MARKETING OFFLINE

So what would happen if social media and the Internet disappeared tomorrow? Not likely, but you never know! Would your business be dead in the water? We've talked about the importance of social media and web presence but, realistically, not everyone will come across your website, so get out there! In fact, there are many customers out there who prefer good ol' fashioned marketing. Here are a few simple, low cost ways to get exposure in your community that don't take much work at all!

The goal with these marketing offline tips is to implement techniques that will continually work for you so that your time, money and energy are dedicated to making Little Sally's ballet costume by hand…or just ordering it off Etsy.

***

IT'S THE LITTLE THINGS

First, marketing does not have to be a wide-scale investment to reach a lot of customers It can be as little as a bumper sticker, carrying pens with your logo, or an identifying item (example: A photographer may carry a coffee mug shaped like a lens). No matter the item it should be identifiable enough to become a conversation starter.

Laundry Tip: Keep professionalism in mind when being in public with an identifier of your company. Road rage never pulled in a customer. Nor did impatience with a receptionist at a professional office.

For many companies, even Internet-based, businesses will find individuals in their community in need of their product or service. By placing these small items into their view in the grocery store line or at soccer practice, the message is getting out there. You may even find potential customers will use these items as conversation starters, which opens up the possibility that you may gain new customers when you're not even in the office!

Keys to "Little Things" Marketing:

- Make sure it is obvious without being a neon sign.

- Be unique in the item you choose.

- Have a response and business card ready when someone inquires about your item.

- Avoid logos all the time. Be a little subtler with an item that demonstrates your business.

I will tell you that I am not above using my kids for marketing through the "little things" approach. One of my businesses is being a wedding and portrait photographer.

When my littlest was born I snatched up as many camera shirts I could find. I mean..who doesn't love a baby? Who doesn't talk to a baby? What a perfect way to strike up conversation. Not to mention..I even went as far as to buy him a play camera to pair with the shirt.

BAM!
Instant conversation starter.

***

BUSINESS CARD DROPPING

The second easy marketing-offline strategy is through good ol' business card dropping. This drives my husband crazy. I'm a chronic business card dropper. Yes, this won't always get the target customer every time but that is okay! The point of business card dropping is to get exposure. What better way to get exposure than through a low-cost, tangible marketing material strategically placed around town? The point of business card dropping is to get exposure.

Keys to Business Card Dropping:

- Always ask the business owner permission to leave business cards in their location. They may have partnerships and relationships with competitors and the placement of your card could potentially disrupt or violate that agreement. Even if no agreement exists, it is in good form to ask permission.

- Identify businesses your target customer frequents for maximum return on time and investment.

- Stay away from competitor businesses unless there is enough variety in products/services that a relationship could be advantageous for both parties involved.

- Make your business card memorable and consistent for branding.

- Ensure your business card has all-important contact information and relays what type of business you are in.

- Leave a card with your check at lunch, or even exchange with the cupcake lady when picking up Little Sally's ballet recital's party goods.

This is definitely another way to exploit, I mean utilize, your children. Consider pairing holiday treat bags for school or sports teams with your business card. Just a nice subtle advertisement to get your company's name in front of the community will do the trick.

When my oldest son was in first grade his class had a Halloween treat party at school. I trotted down to the store, gathered supplies to make skeleton hands out of rubber gloves and popcorn. I slipped a business card on the "bracelet" of the hand.

Oh snap!

Just like that, my name was in front of a bunch of parents running their own home businesses. End-of-year wrap up was coming up and many were in need of business consulting. Who do you think they checked out?

Timing. Exploitation…cough..utilization. Business.

***

EXPOS, FAIRS, CONFERENCES, OH MY!

Another relatively easy marketing-offline strategy is through attending local industry expos, fairs and conferences. These places allow for networking with other similar industry vendors, but specifically target the market that you have if you choose the right event! The key to using these events is to create and/or grow your customer list. By having incentives such as discounts, freebies or door prizes in exchange for potential customer information you can seamlessly convert this in-person marketing strategy to an online marketing-strategy.

Keys to Expos/Fairs:

- Obtain potential customer information at the event for follow up.

- Make sure you follow up!!!

- Incentivize potential customers to provide their contact information (and to gain attention) through the use of a giveaway, door prize or discount.

- Take appropriate marketing materials. Run of the mill business cards won't work. Make it specific to the event with a proper call to action and deadline for those that receive it to act.

***

CUSTOMER REFERRAL PROGRAM

Also consider using your customers as walking, talking billboards for your business. By giving them the tools to do so and an incentive, you can create a trickle down marketing campaign. There are two main ways to do this: formally and informally.

For a formal referral program, it is just like it is titled: formal. It consists of a set of formal requirements that you provide to your customers, telling them what they have to gain and how to cash in on their incentive.

Examples:

#1 Provide your customers with referral cards containing a blank to fill in their information. Encourage them to deliver the cards to friends and family. When their referee comes in with the card the customer will be credited. After X credits they will receive X incentive.

#2 Provide your customers a customer information card or sign in sheet upon entrance to the place of business with a spot that allows for them to write in the referring party. Encourage the customer to remind their friends and family to fill in their name. When the referee comes and fills in the spot, the customer will be credited. After X credits they will receive X incentive.

For an informal referral program, drive the referrals through custom and personalized follow-ups and great customer service. This can be done by ensuring customers were satisfied with their product/service and demonstrating appreciation for their business.

Examples:

#1 At the end of year, send a personalized thank you to the customer as a way to keep your name in front of them for potential referrals.

#2 Whenever customers send referrals, be sure to send a thank you note and an incentive (such as a gift certificate or discount).

***

CUSTOMER THANK YOUS

Never underestimate the strength of a simple thank you. Sometimes a handwritten note or a follow –up email will cement the customer experience. Depending on the scale of business, customer gifts may perfectly finish the experience and further the business relationship.

Tips to Customer Thank Yous:

- Handwrite if possible. Personal touches go a long way. If your handwriting is as bad as mine (I should've been a doctor okay...) then consider outsourcing the personalization.

- Include the customer's name instead of a standard stock thank you.

- Brand your thank you note with logo and contact information.

- Send the thank you within a couple weeks of the customer's purchase of your product/service.

- Do NOT put an incentive in the thank you note. Let it be a thank you. Reserve the incentive for later.

Laundry Tip: Don't forget to collect customer info for other personalized contact measures such as birthday postcards.

***

GIVING BACK TO THE COMMUNITY

Let me preface this by saying I'm not advising you to give back to the community solely to obtain customers. The primary reason for giving back to the community should be to, well, give back. I am merely recommending this as a way to obtain community attention and widespread branding recognition. Every business should strive to keep up their physical presence in the local community at the same time they are building their online presence.

Some Ways to Give Back:

- Host an event – Host a local event to engage the community with your charitable giving. Events include canned food drives, winter weather coat collections, back-to-school supply gathering, etc.

- Solicit those in need (quietly) – Don't advertise a free product or service. Rather, use pre-existing marketing channels to put out feelers for those in need of a specific service.

- Solicit those in need (loudly) - Put it out for the community to see that you are seeking a way to give back.

- Thank your customers – Simply thank your current and past customers with an individualized thank you. No tricks. No gimmicks. Just a thank you.

Laundry Tip: Try giving back through organizations that you are closely connected to (children's hobbies or sports) or have a heart for (cancer, disease, cause, etc.).

As a cancer survivor, giving back to the community through organizations supporting other patients and survivors is extremely important to the mission of my business and my heart. When I give my heart is to give. If there is a return on the investment then great. If not, at least I gave with my whole heart.

Living in a military community results in many spouse fairs and events. One fall, after I had just moved my business (again!), I donated to a military spouse expo for a free consultation session. I never heard from the winner. Fastforward two years later. The winner was digging through boxes and found my business card from her winnings. This person got in contact with me and was regretful of wasting the item they had won. Since then she has engaged in my online community and has become a large network source that provides a constant supply of referrals. My heart was fulfilled with no expectation of return. While not a direct return, rewards have been reaped down the road.

***

LOCAL ADVERTISEMENTS

Advertisements occur around you all the time. I could insert some statistic here that is amazing and encourages you to advertise, but you already know that the right advertisement is effective in promoting your business. Yup! That's how much we are around advertisements in our daily lives, whether subtle or in our faces. Some of these include radio, television, theater previews, stationary billboards, moving billboards, etc.

Tips to Placing Local Ads:

- Say who you are, what you do and how to get in contact with you

- Make it memorable but not annoying or in-your-face

- Reiterate contact information

- Consider pairing an incentive

- Evaluate the times/places ads will be seen (middle of the night on a television station may reap lower amounts of response than during the day)

Laundry Tip: Weigh the cost versus the benefit. Sometimes a well-placed advertisement in a less popular medium will attract the type of customer to which your business is catered.. A newspaper ad might be a more cost-effective measure than local television advertisements if you are unable to afford prime time television time.

***

DISCOUNT INCENTIVE PROGRAMS

Who doesn't love a good bargain? Obviously a ton of people, since there are various coupon websites, along with VIP/Coupon books and cards sold as fundraisers popping up everywhere. However, this is the one marketing option, next to print advertisements, that I strongly caution evaluating the return on investment and potential damage to brand. It can work phenomenally, as it may bring a high quantity of customers in your doors, but be prepared to have the proper amount of products or manpower for services to fulfill the resulting demand.

Always place a deadline on the promotion. Without a deadline, there is no sense of urgency for the customers to spend the money. Design the promotion to attract those valuable long-term customers. If you've provided a good service or product and the ultimate customer service experience, the promotion should only have been the hook to get them in the door. The remainder should be what is driving the repeat business.

Laundry Tip: Wasted time on repeat discount customers is wasted profits and energy that could have been focused on target customers.

Like anything else in business, inform the customer and state all policies and exclusions on the offer. It is also beneficial to ensure there is an appropriate and efficient way to track and confirm any pre-purchased incentives.

Don't run these types of promotions too often and don't allow them to be combined with any other promotion. The continual repetitive promotions will devalue the brand and replace your target customers with a set of customers that you don't necessarily want as your primary source of business.

Laundry Tip: Determine whether promotions like this will retain new customers or they are one-time deal seekers. The lack of valuable customer retention results in a low return on investment.

On the business front, keep the current promotions on the business calendar and a copy of promotions on hand for reference.

***

BUILD BUSINESS RELATIONSHIPS

Getting other small business owners on your side is probably one of the smartest marketing moves you can make. And who knows? Along the way you might make a friend! There are tons of small business owners in any populated area and I'm willing to bet the majority are parents or plan to be. Besides the personal benefits, getting in with local businesses will help build credibility for your business, reduce marketing load, and increase efficiency in marketing as the target customer will be directly confronted with your name and information.

Tips to Building Business Relationships:

- Tailor marketing materials to the target customer. Avoid standard business cards.

- Provide an incentive to the customer of the business establishment that will be distributing your materials.

Laundry Tip: Pair solicitation calls with a memorable item to be remembered. Examples include donuts, free pens/stationary, and samples.

Tips to Approaching Business Owners:

- Approach the business owner with a mutually beneficial relationship in mind. Never approach asking someone to do your bidding.

- Never go during a busy time. If they are a restaurant owner, avoid meal rush times.

- Always call or email ahead of time to inquire about a good time to talk. Imagine how busy your day is and remember a courtesy call will go a long way.

- Always follow up with a thank you even if the business owner has declined a relationship.

***

BE BOLD!

Always be bold when you're being asked about what you do. Even at the doctor's office when the forms ask what your occupation is. Fill it out with your business name, position and contact information. Go up and give out your business card. Never shy away from an opportunity to discuss what you do.

Laundry Tip: Don't be overbearing. Be bold but not obnoxious. Be in tune with people's body language so you don't drive them away.

***

No matter the marketing plan you take, always evaluate periodically to determine whether your investment of time and money is having any return. Without a return on investment, your marketing is going nowhere, and in turn, your business is going nowhere as well. You'd go further by rocking fast on Little Timmy's rocking horse. Seriously. Corporations spend billions of dollars on marketing firms to do research and evaluation of marketing campaigns. You may be smaller and doing your own analysis, but ignoring the results and return will leave your business in the dust and inefficient.

Marketing Language Tips

- **Avoid the use of the word "I". Make it about your customer.**

  Not: I will give you X product/service.
  Use: You will receive X product/service.

- **Use deadline statements**

  Only X left! Only X hours remaining!
  Ends in X hours.

- **Use the Value Meal Effect Method**

  See the Pricing & Sales Chapter

CHAPTER SEVEN:

OUTSOURCING

Outsourcing is the practice of delegating tasks to outside businesses to handle work that is part of running your business. The most popular types of outsourcing include accounting, payroll processing, and marketing. Most people think of out-of-country hired assistance when outsourcing is discussed, when in fact many small businesses outsource to the community. Don't put up a stonewall to outsourcing. Think of the moments when you've been trying to answer last minute urgent customer emails by smartphone, holding a screaming baby in one arm with spit up dripping down your arm. Bet you wish in that moment you had outsourced some tasks to free yourself up, huh?

***

WHY TO OUTSOURCE

So you know you need help. You know you want help. But what will give you the extra shove to outsource? How about saving money and increasing efficiency? As a business owner and parent these are two important aspects that should always in the forefront of your mind when making business decisions. This fact makes the decision FOR outsourcing that more hard-hitting.

Saves Money

At the very heart of business is **(cue music)**... money! But more than just physical money. It's the money lost when you spend time on frivolous tasks. Busy does not necessarily equal better.

You can make yourself busy all day long, but if you're not moving forward then you're just wasting time, money and energy. You can be losing time, money and customers by being too busy with the wrong tasks. It's time to get efficient, whether it is through automation or outsourcing. Some business owners confuse being busy with being successful. It all boils down to what you're busy with. Are you busy with mundane tasks that give little return on investment? Or are they tasks that reap a huge reward? If it's the former, you're losing money and time...and you need to look at outsourcing. If it's the latter, you may still benefit from outsourcing but do not necessarily need it.

Laundry Tip: Outsourcing will only save you money if you do your research and outsource the proper tasks. Outsourcing everything may produce a loss.

Think of it this way. You, as the business owner, have a value of hundreds per hour for your time. Some tasks are only worth a five or ten dollar bill at a time. They are still needed in the business, but do not have the same value. To get into the nitty-gritty of numbers, let's figure this up. For your global to-do list tasks, figure out how much time you'll save by outsourcing and compare this to what you have identified as your typical hourly rate. For instance, if you are an attorney that charges $250 an hour and you are spending three to five hours per month working on payroll. A payroll service or bookkeeper could be outsourced to at an investment of $100-300, depending on size of work. Further, these outsourced companies have the supports already in place and are trained on the programs needed to be utilized to fulfill the work requirement, thus decreasing the amount of time spent on the task.

Example:

5 hours work by your own hands x $250 = $1250
3.5 hours of outsourced work x $100 = $350

Results in a savings of $900 + 5 hours of work

Increases Efficiency

Companies that are operating a on a limited budget will find themselves piling tasks on top of the workloads of existing employees. Piling on the work will decrease efficiency and productivity in daily tasks, as well as the "piled on" tasks. In turn, this will end up costing the company time and money. This time and money could be spent elsewhere, such as marketing, to propel your business forward.

Further, outsourcing to a professional trained in the particular task will increase efficiency as it may result in more accurate results or a quicker turn around for the customer.

Frees up your time

As a working parent, time is important. There are only so many hours a day that you can have (or want to have) your children being cared for by others. Outsourcing will work to free up time to allow for more attendances at t-ball games or just merely kicking back and watching Barney for the one-millionth time.

***

WHAT TO OUTSOURCE

Outsourcing can especially help a business on tasks that require specific expertise such as payroll, marketing and web design. Other tasks to outsource are ones that have a low rate of return on investment of time including cleaning, filing, and routine maintenance of the office and equipment.

Payroll and Accounting Services

Many services that offer payroll and accounting services are efficient and cost-effective. Deciding to outsource between these two takes a bit of understanding about your business needs and investment. Businesses that require more in depth tax assistance may require the retention of a Certified Public Accountant, whereas others may simply need payroll services. Some businesses may even need both. Seek out the type of company within your budget that will meet your needs to maximize outsourcing.

Cleaning and Repairs

Taking time to clean and repair the office are probably extremely inefficient wastes of time. The amount of return on your time investment is well worth the outsourcing cost. Cleaning services are widespread and competitive in pricing.

Laundry Tip: Consider having someone come into your home to do personal cleaning to help lighten the 'balancing act' load between work and home. And if your office is your home, then the answer is quite obvious!

Marketing

Despite all the efficient ways to self-market included in this book, outsourcing the marketing aspect can lift a huge load off your shoulders. There are firms out there who specialize in marketing and have extensive channels in place to maximize marketing for your money.

Outsourcing doesn't necessarily have to involve an actual person. You can outsource your marketing to electronic programs that can auto-publish content (see Automation), but still require an input of information.

Web and Blog Design

Thanks to ever-evolving technology, there are so many inexpensive options for professional web and blog designs out there. However, the issue isn't the cost. It is the time and functionality. Even if you are an expert in this area, you may not have the time to dedicate to your own site between customers.

Virtual Support

Through the use of local phone centers and virtual help desks, you can receive virtual support with a variety of tasks. Local phone centers can provide customer service support on an as-needed basis. Virtual assistants provide administrative, technical or other supports. Both type of services work on a contractual basis and their support is delivered online or over the telephone.

Laundry Tip: If outsourcing a task that has a "voice," ensure that it is similar to yours and speaks your brand. For example, if you hire a social media marketer, their posts should be phrased and delivered in the same manner as you would do it.

A major benefit to virtual support staffs is the low cost of overhead, as business owners typically do not have to provide the equipment for this staff to work. A tradeoff is the potential for a decline in standards of service or product. Further, you lose a bit of your personal knowledge and interpersonal relationships and rapport with customers. It is important to factor in some time for oversight when outsourcing virtually, especially for those interacting directly with customers.

***

HOW DO I KNOW IF I SHOULD OUTSOURCE?

This is relatively straightforward. Answer a few of the following questions. If any of them have the answer of "yes," you should look into outsourcing. If you have an answer of "maybe," then keep outsourcing on the global to-do list to think about in the future. If you've answered "no" to all of them, then either you're supermom or you need to see why you have the answer of no. Most business owners outsource at least one thing, even if it is simple automation. That is outsourcing, too!

Questions to ask yourself:

- Are there tasks draining the life out of you?

- Are there tasks draining the time out of your day?

- What about tasks that you absolutely enjoy but have a low return on investment for?

- Are there tasks that need done regularly that you'd rather not think about?

I can tell you for sure that a telltale sign of knowing you need to outsource is when you find yourself past midnight, staring blankly at the wall with Baby Einstein still running on the television. I even think that the water may still have been running in the bathroom sink…who knows. I was so tired and worn out. Right then and there I knew for sure I needed help.

I was tired.
I was rundown.
I was an irritable mom.
I was an unproductive business owner.

If you ever get to this point run to the closest bed first, then get up and make a plan to outsource.

***

HOW TO OUTSOURCE

Okay, so you've probably been convinced that outsourcing some aspects of your business is a good idea, especially those in which you are inefficient or lack the proper capability. But now you need to figure out how to outsource appropriately.

What is your business built on?

It all starts with taking a look at the value that you can offer to customers and where to focus your efforts. Value is typically tied to the core of the business, where the mission of the business rests.

For example, a consulting business has a core mission to consult for other businesses. All the extras such as paperwork and payroll are not part of the core mission. They are vital to keep it running, but are not part of the core aspect of business. If those items are put off a day, the business will not fall apart. If those items are outsourced, the customer probably will not care or even know. But if the consulting aspect is delayed or outsourced, the customers will receive a lackluster customer experience and ultimately seek help elsewhere. Be mindful about which tasks you outsource, and you could improve the profitability and efficiency of your business.

Making the move

To make the move toward outsourcing can be scary for a small business owner who has done it all since the beginning, or wants to have their hands in all pots. The advantages of outsourcing, after researching, will have great advantages over disadvantages. However, commit little by little. It may take some time to find a good fit, especially when using someone to handle customer service. If you have staff in place, it helps to incrementally work toward outsourcing to let them adjust to the idea and express any concerns.

Be wise in outsourcing

If you have the time and money to do a task, then you probably should be doing it. When it starts invading on your time with Little Timmy or the core mission of your business, then you can start to outsource. Don't outsource merely to free up more time and burn money. That money can be invested elsewhere to expand and grow the business.

Keys to Outsourcing

- Don't outsource brainstorming activities

  Keep all brainstorming and innovative creation activities in house to maintain your brand and business.

- Try fixing it yourself

Check to see if it's just inefficiency on your part that needs fixing.

- Research automation

  Is it a task that you only need minor help on? Will automation fix that for you?

- Consider your cost of doing business

  Can you actually afford to outsource? Will it only require a few more hours in your day or are you completely lost without outsourcing?

- Be informed

  Enter into a contractual outsourcing relationship fully informed of all expectations, responsibilities and costs. Some outsourcing functions may only require hourly or part-time attention and allow for the burden of cost to be considered as a variable cost instead of a fixed business cost.

- Do NOT outsource your core mission.

  Once it is out the door it is no longer yours and your customers will follow.

***

HOW TO FIND COMPANIES TO OUTSOURCE TO

Finding a reputable and trustworthy company is a key piece in the outsourcing puzzle. Finding someone to handle tasks that impact your business and livelihood requires some work on your part. Use referrals arising out of networking relationships, social media platforms and the plethora of freelance job sites available on the Internet.

Besides marketing assistance, networking with local professionals will provide a source of potential referrals for outsourcing. Reach out to key trusted network professionals and inquire as to any recommendations. By having a personal endorsement, there is a lower probability of issues as long as it comes from a trusted contact.

Laundry Tip: Only take recommendations from trusted network sources. If you have any doubts about the source then reconsider the outsourcing recommendation as well.

As always, good ol' social media saves the day. Simply putting out an inquiry can result in a mass amount of response. The trick is finding the time and discernment to sift through all inquiries. LinkedIn and other professional social media platforms can provide professional recommendations as well.

Also consider taking on an intern from a local community college or university to work on these tasks for you. You may be able to provide some credit to them and provide an experience for the intern. Most internships that are in exchange for credit will have oversight from the host educational institution, and may not allow for compensation.

Laundry Tip: Free help is always awesome for bottom line! Even better if that free help is coupled with giving back to the local community by way of experience.

No matter how the company or individual to outsource to is found, always seek recommendations and resumes to determine whether they have the right education, experience, capabilities, qualifications and professionalism.

CHAPTER EIGHT:

SALES & PRICING

aking sales is the key to turning a profit in business. While marketing gets your name out there, it is up to you to pull customers in the door. In Chapter 2 we discussed business and marketing planning but didn't get to the nitty-gritty of sales. This is done through effective marketing campaigns (which we've discussed in depth), converting inquiries into customers, appropriate pricing strategies, and increasing prices. You're probably thinking, "Well, I've got sales down. I can close the deal."

Okay but listen.

Is your pricing sealing the deal *for* you? Is it helping to grease the customer wheels? If it's not, then you're burning time and money. Implementing effective and efficient sales techniques and pricing measures will decrease your time and increase your efficiency immensely.

***

TURNING INQUIRIES INTO CUSTOMERS

Getting potential customers to inquire is half the battle. To win that battle work your social media, networking and other marketing techniques. The other half is turning them into customers, whether immediately or down the road. Your goal with customer inquiries is (and should be) about obtaining customer information and using that information to convert these inquiries into booking customers.

I visualize this as though they are a customer standing in my foyer. They've come to my website, they have inquired, I have responded. They are hanging out in the foyer of my house. My goal now is not to keep them in the foyer, but to pull them into my living room (or as a business, into my office!).

Or you could visualize it as your two-year old throwing a fit in the supermarket foyer. You want nothing more than to get them out of the store and into the car. Persuasion. Incentive. Gritting teeth and making it happen without making the waves higher.

Our entire goal with these five methods is to pull customers that are hanging out in the foyer into your living room, and then turn them into loyal current and future customers. These tips will help get those customers into the living room and sitting comfortably on your sofa.

Customer Questionnaire

Instead of an email address or customer information form, create a questionnaire. Have your customers engage in the inquiry process with specific questions such as the date, type of service or product requested, and a personal fact about themselves. This information will allow you to answer with a personalized response that aids in helping to humanize yourself on the other end of the inquiry. This will also allow you, as the business owner, to start brainstorming the details of a future transaction.

Send Information Immediately

In an age where everyone "wants it now," give it to them now…or as close as possible. Customer inquiries should be at the top of the response list. No customers, no income, no business. Commit to getting a response out as quickly as possible. You can do this by either having it come to your phone, or have scheduled email-checking times throughout the day. If you opt to call them back, call as quickly as possible. Keep your background free of noise for easy conversation.

Also, always have your information quickly on hand through a template email, informational page on the website or a PDF/virtual document version of your customer guide. Sending information by hand is best sent during scheduled office hours (or school hours if they coincide). Consider an automated option to providing information without requiring a handwritten response each time.

Laundry Tip: The "want it now" attitude of today's customers can be detrimental to moms. Always ensure boundaries and expectations are set to customers. And always automate for full information and response to clients as soon as possible.

Add to Customer List

Customer lists are gold. Absolute gold. You often hear of companies having non-compete clauses and requiring confidentiality of customer lists. This is because customer lists are EASY to market to because you already have them in the door (visualize the foyer/living room scenario above). Use a newsletter service to customize a newsletter with your branding logo and colors. This will allow you to set up for auto sending and tracking of email recipient interaction. Anything that is automated will save you valuable time!

Send a Follow Up

Always send a follow up, whether there has been interaction about a booking/sale or not. Always let the customer know that you're still thinking of them. This can easily be automated by adding them to a distribution list that will automatically send a follow up in the future. Don't forget to send an end of the year follow up/ thank you. This is essentially free marketing. You've already received their information and added them to the list, so why not work at pulling them into your living room?

Incentivize & Call to Action

In an effort to get these customers out of our foyer and into our living room, we need to incentivize and "call" them in. Your communications should use psychological words such as "only" and "gift" so the customer feels that the communication is just for them, and that the incentive you're offering them is exclusively theirs. Even if you are marketing to a large group of potential customers, it is still possible to structure your communications so that each recipient feels that you are speaking only to them. You can put this technique into action if they don't book after X number of months. Keep your name in front of them. Put yourself right into their email inbox.

Remember, all marketing takes some time. Just because you aren't hearing back immediately doesn't mean they don't want you or that your marketing isn't working. Give it time, and then give it the extra effort of follow up. The goal with all these tips is to demonstrate to customers that you desire and value their business. Don't give up. Business will not happen in the foyer; it happens in the living room.

***

PRICING FOR SALES

Get to know the basics, understand your customer's psychology, and implement strategies to sell your product or service. In the end you can achieve higher sales, fulfillment as an entrepreneur and stability as a business owner.

Basics of Pricing

Just like anything else, you need to know the basics. Gotta crawl before you walk and walk before you run. You will need to go through the painful basics. By taking the time now to make an educated formulation of pricing, you will save yourself time, money, and energy.

- Know your market

  What can your market REALLY handle? And I mean truly handle. I hear so many people tell me their market is saturated with small businesses. WAKE UP! This is true everywhere. That doesn't mean you can't price yourself appropriately. Remember, not every small business owner in your geographical area is your competitor. Identify the true competitors and your target customer.

- Know your competitors

  Who are your competitors? These are other businesses that provide the same skill level and market brand of your product or service. Figure out who your competitors are and what they charging. Balance your price points against your competitors' price points.

- Know your target customer

What are their demographics, occupations, socio-economic influences? Do you have a specific idea of who they are? Or is your marketing targeting a vague audience with hopes that your target customer will walk in the door?

- Know your overhead

  This is so crucial and pretty much one of the main reasons why you can't simply look to competitors for their prices. Everyone has a different amount of overhead. In order to successfully maintain any business, pricing should set so that even at the lowest sale you are breaking even.

Laundry Tip: I prefer to have a buffer on my lowest price point, but a general rule is to use your break-even point, especially if you are trying to penetrate the market.

- What is your desired income?

  This also varies from one business owner to another. Again, you don't want to be working for free. Your time away from your everyday life and family is worth something. Identify your appropriate income based on your education, skill, time in business and what you value your time as. Keep in mind a self-valuation may not always be accurate.

Laundry Tip: Seek out a business consultant to determine a fair and objective value of your time and skillset.

- Value yourself

People place more value in services and goods they cannot provide or create for themselves. The majority of your customers probably are not adept at creating your product or delivering your service, which is why they come to you. Imagine this: you absolutely stink at sewing (*I am raising my hand!*) so you have no qualms about going to Etsy and purchasing a dress for Little Sally for $XX. But if you know how to sew and have the equipment, you probably won't run out and spend more than $X, if you decide to spend anything at all for a product/service you can provide yourself. It's the same way with delivering your product or service in your business. There are customers out there who are unable or unwilling to recreate what you can provide and, therefore, are willing to pay what you are worth.

Laundry Tip: Don't wash out prospective clients who want to value you by giving them a generic version of you.

Don't get overwhelmed. The most important thing is to ensure that you are effectively pricing for yourself. Pricing, like anything else, is not set in stone. As a business owner, YOU are the boss. You can make changes as you see fit. And you should make changes as you grow as a business owner, gain feedback from customers and as the economic market and demand changes.

***

DOING THE NUMBERS

Before pricing a product or service you must understand the total cost of production and distribution. Understanding the total cost allows you to look at the margin or profit that you want to obtain. The costs include development, research, manufacturing, distribution, labor and overhead. These categories of cost can be broken down further into time, skill, sales commissions, advertising, packaging, promotional materials, business travel, and other related costs. *See the Cost of Doing Business section for more information.*

***

PRICING STRATEGIES

Pricing strategies must complement the business's overall goals and strategies. Price strategies will differ based on the owner's business objectives. For example, to achieve market penetration, a business owner may decide to price the product or service below the competition. This approach is used to gain market share and to establish entry into a new market.

When determining a pricing strategy, you need to take profit into extra consideration. Profit is the amount left after production costs and non-production costs are subtracted from gross revenue. Growth of a business can only come with reasonable profits that allow you a reasonable return on investment. In addition, some of the cash flow and profits must be turned back into the business to sustain inventories, accounts receivable, capital equipment purchases, and other assets. Depending on the nature of the business, a certain amount of asset structure is needed to support sales. The larger the sales level, the larger the asset structure needed to support the sales growth. This requires that some of the profit be returned to the business in order to facilitate growth.

This is the meat of where efficiency and driving sales to what you want them to be will come from. THIS is important so that you can spend more time giving your customer an experience and service than chasing after their dollars. This will also allow you to spend more time with your family and provide a great income for support. There are numerous pricing strategies a business can use to complement the stated business goals. The most common are market penetration, skimming, neutral and follower pricing.

Market penetration

This aggressive strategy accomplishes pretty much what it is called..penetration to the market. This may include pricing a same or similar product/service below the competition in order to gain a foothold on the market. A downfall may be lower profits in the beginning but can pay dividends as the customer base is established.

Neutral Position

This strategy allows for prices to be set by identifying competitors and their pricing structure. Neutral positioning is the most safe and secure strategy to implement, as it will carry a business throughout all lifecycles. In this strategy the CODB may need to be decreased in order to maintain a decent profit margin.

Skimming

This strategy invokes the mental image of the time I had to fish my day planner out of the toilet. The price of your product or service starts relatively high when it comes into the market but then lowers over time. By adopting this strategy you are essentially skimming the market demand. This strategy helps new businesses gain high profits upon entrance into market, however, when other similar products/services enter the market or the product/service becomes matured and the price is then lowered. This type of strategy is most beneficial for technological markets and products with strong patents in place.

Follower pricing

This pricing strategy is exactly what it states. You are following the leaders that you've identified as your direct competition. This strategy takes a reactive approach on the basis that the leaders will maintain their position as opposed to taking notice your pricing and respond with lower pricing. This pricing strategy requires a low cost of doing business in order to have a higher profit margin. If you are unable to cut costs and maintain an optimal product or service then the competition will exploit your pricing that can result in a detriment to your business.

***

PSYCHOLOGY OF CUSTOMERS

When it comes to customers there is so much more than just providing a quality product at a good price. There is a psychology to the way information is presented, branding is displayed and pricing is relayed. Customers do not want to underwhelmed or overwhelmed. Providing too little or too much information can be detrimental. It's kind of like the story of the Three Little Bears. One bed was too soft, another was too hard. But one was just right. That "just right" bed is where you want to rest and settle your customers into with pricing and presentation.

Don't overwhelm your customers

I've learned pricing through practice and formal education, but it wasn't until I noticed how I as a consumer am driven to purchase certain packages that I realized the appeal of having just enough options.

When starting out in my own business, I remember dropping into the pedicure chair and, quite frankly, I just wanted someone to rub my swollen, preggo feet. However, when presented with the menu of pedicure packages I was OVERWHELMED with choices. I ended up not even reading the menu and selected the "middle" package because I figured I would get a "good enough" pedicure without paying for the most expensive. Right then I thought about and realized how often customers are overwhelmed with choices and just default to what is "good enough" but not "too expensive."

Don't underwhelm your customers

Lack of choices can lead to customers reluctantly choosing a product or service (thereby reducing their experience with you) or not wanting to order at all. Displaying enough products or services to customers will aid a customer in feeling informed and more comfortable with their choices from the menu you're providing. The balance between underwhelming and overwhelming can be difficult. Think about when you've entered a restaurant and the menu was the size of an encyclopedia. You probably defaulted to an item you typically eat elsewhere just because it was safe and didn't require too much research. However, if the menu provided next to nothing, you probably felt underwhelmed and disappointed in the limited selections.

Here's a perfect example! Remember back to when you were expecting (whether biologically, adoption or through marriage) to have a child enter into your home. The amount of 'stuff' that was desired to help the child acclimate to the surroundings was overwhelming. Typically, parents turn to friends/family for recommendations on how to narrow down the choices while still providing enough choices that you aren't underwhelmed.

SECRET WEAPON: *The Value Meal Effect*

Each of the previously discussed strategies need to be delicately handled with the psychology of the client. Customers like to have the option to choose between similar items based either on the price, quality or specific characteristics, so you should also offer an alternative option. A tried and true method of how these options work and how to predict which option your customer will go for is easily seen in the real world. Imagine you're pulling up to a drive through and you order your value meal. They ask, "Do you want that small, medium or large?" Which do you typically order? Medium! Society has engrained in us this idea that middle range is best. Less is bad, and more is too much. People are comfortable in the middle. It is important to remember this when bundling together your products or services.

Laundry Tip: The entire goal is to get your customers to buy the product or service that you want them to buy. By using the Value Meal Effect psychology, you will guide them to purchase along your plan.

***

HOW DO I RAISE MY PRICES?

As business trucks along, there comes the need and desire for increased profits. In order to raise your prices you must have already established a pricing strategy. This strategy is the plan that allowed you to calculate the cost of doing business and evaluate local competitor pricing. There are many ways to raise prices while retaining current customers and still attracting new customers.

- **The Quarter Method**

Every quarter, incrementally increase your pricing. By using this method you will not provide sticker-shock to clients.

- **The Value Meal Effect (Revisited)**

  Shift around your customer options while maintaining the Value Meal Effect. By taking what was originally your goal (medium meal) product or service and shifting it to the bottom, top to the middle, you can add on a new large value meal. This is kind of like climbing a ladder…with a Big Mac and a side of fries in your hand. The goal of raising prices is to continually increase sales but keep customers at the same time. This method can be done in conjunction with The Quarter Method for a structured and effective way to move yourself and your business along.

- **Upsell**

  By offering add on products or services, you can easily increase profit revenue and provide the customer with the experience that suits their needs. Include the Upselling in your standard sales workflow (See Chapter 4 for workflow).

Laundry Tip: Only offer additional services that they actually need. Constant upselling can quickly turn to nagging and become a turnoff completely.

***

Overall, pricing can be tricky but will pay dividends (literally) if given the appropriate time and forethought. If pricing is just thrown together with disregard for market competitors or common sales price the business will sink. If the pricing is thoroughly researched and implemented strategically it can become one of the greatest marketing assets your company will have. (Psst....if it's working for you it'll free up time. Maybe enough for you to sneak in that afternoon nap!)

CHAPTER NINE:

TAKING TIME OFF

Running a business shouldn't be all…business. When you have a family, it is a requirement that you take time for yourself and your family. Hey, even taking a vacation without the family sounds good some days, but I digress. The biggest myth about small business owners is the idea that if you take off, your business will lose profits, fall apart or both. I personally think you need to take time off or else the pressures and stress can reach so high that you end up causing more stress on yourself, your family and your business, resulting in negative consequences.

TAKE A TIME OUT!

SERIOUSLY!

So get the myth that your entire entrepreneurial career is over if you take a few days off out of your mind. It won't happen if you put the right supports into place.

In fact, the benefits of taking time off can pile up higher than the negatives if you actually hop on that plane. It is proven, just like during regular workdays, that productivity increases after a break from the routine. Also, business owners who take time off to clear their minds actually tend to produce more innovative approaches. Kind of like how you're hit with a genius marketing idea when you're in the shower, soap in hair and can't reach your phone to jot it down. Getting away refreshes the mind so you can develop more innovative ideas to grow your business with.

So take it from the experts. Getting away is good for you. With advanced planning, communication with clients, getting help and a few other "time out" supports, your visions of dipping toes in the sand (or just a simple uninterrupted nap) will become a reality.

***

PLAN IN ADVANCE

Schedule. Like everything else (if you need a refresher check out the chapter on getting tasks done) schedule in your vacations and time off. Be selective in the scheduling, as you obviously do not want to schedule during busy seasons or during the height of a customer relationship.

Laundry Tip: Set up a program that interconnects with all electronic calendars (phone, computers, etc.) for convenience.

If your industry is the type to have extended customer relationships requiring your specific attention, be sure to inform the client ahead of time of any previously scheduled vacations. If your customer relationship fulfillment allows for contribution by another equivalent be sure that your customer contract includes a clause that identifies a substitute is allowed. If the customer relationship does not allow for contribution then be sure to inform customers of the scheduled out-of-office dates.

***

COMMUNICATE WITH YOUR CUSTOMERS

Just as informing customers of a scheduled absence is critical, educating them with what to expect during that time is equally as crucial. By frontloading communication outlining the dates of absence, supports in place in case they need assistance and advisement of a suggested deadline for response upon return, you will assist in alleviating the anxiety of customers. This education will enhance the customer experience and increase their trust in your business abilities.

If you have multiple children you will appreciate this analogy. My then two-year old used to inform me that she was going to poke her four-month old brother in the head prior to committing the act. This allowed for me to communicate and act in a preventative manner and also to be there if the results turned disastrous. Which they always did. This is the same with clients. Give them forewarning of the poke so they aren't surprised when they contact your office and are greeted with disturbing news that you're sailing the Bahamas with fruity drink in hand.

Laundry Tip: Don't worry too much that customers will be insulted or perceive you as incompetent if you take a vacation. Most (note: I said most) customers are reasonable people with families of their own. They just want a heads up in a professional manner to keep all sailing smooth (kind of like that cruise you should be on...).

***

GET HELP

This is probably the most obvious tip, but it may be one of the hardest. Letting go of full control of your baby. Your business. Your livelihood. Just imagine it like you're having a babysitter for the business. Treat it as such by providing all pertinent information and outlining expectations for the replacement.

If you have employees already, you're about halfway there! Hopefully you've already taken it upon yourself to begin delegating tasks; after all, that *is* why you're paying them. If you haven't at least been introducing other employees to your tasks then you need to immediately. Even if you have absolutely no plans to sip piña coladas or go dancing in the rain, what if something happened to you or kids? What if you needed to be away because of an emergency?

Laundry Tip: In the process of delegation, you will find yourself creating a manual for the employee. Identify inefficient workflow steps or missing actions that should be taken. Reintegrate these into your "to-do" lists and everyday workflow.

If you don't currently have someone who is immersed in the business on a regular basis, it may be a bit nerve-wracking and tiring to train them, but will be well worth it for the reasons mentioned above. Especially if you are a sole business owner and operator, the replacement may be a foreign individual to your business.

Keep in mind that whether they work as a current employee or not someone who is not normally in charge of your operation on a daily basis may have no understanding as to what constitutes an emergency and may feel the need to jump the phone call gun to touch base with you. This completely and utterly wastes the entire idea of a vacation and taking a "time out." Outline the expectations as to what constitutes an emergency. Be very specific and clear as to the plan of action for a variety of circumstances.

After relaying all expectations and training materials, inquire to your replacement as to whether they possess any concerns about being in control during your absence. Keep an open mind and informatively respond to reassure this person.

Laundry Tip: Approach your replacement with an understanding attitude. Ruling with an iron fist due to stress or apprehension will result in less communication and an increased probability of issues in your absence.

Lastly, have a couple trial runs to see how the replacement acts under pressure. Take a couple hours for the spa or to just wander around Target for a few hours. Even consider taking some time to remotely work (catch up on some global to-do list tasks) while the replacement handles the office. This allows you to either get ahead or take some time for you and prime the replacement a bit before the big absence.

***

NETWORK

Just as networking is important for marketing, it is also important for being able to take time off. When a network is built with solid, trustworthy and responsible small business owners in the local community, the customers and business owners both win. The small business owners are able to refer out customers in times of need. And trust me…vacation is a time of need.

Laundry Tip: Consider a referral fee whenever referrals are made. Keep track and make sure the relationship is a two-way street. Be sure to thank your network for their assistance during any out of office absences.

***

LIMIT YOUR COMMUNICATION

Limit your communication with the office and customers during your absence. It one hundred percent defeats the purpose of going on vacation if you will be at everyone's beck and call. Your children won't appreciate you missing their cannon balls into the pool while your nose is buried in mobile emails. But if you absolutely have a need to work, whether it's due to your control issues or a customer demand, limit yourself and make a schedule.

Laundry Tip: Practice limiting communication while you are still at home. Stick to office hours to avoid getting into a habit.

If you find you must, work X amount of hours during the morning to clear communications for the day. If you get away geographically but not mentally, then there will be no benefits to reap or any balancing of family.

***

AUTOMATE

Ahh! Automation again! Oh yes, technology nowadays allows for you to work while not working. Scheduling social media updates, newsletters, and publishing of blog posts will help to alleviate a lot of the stress associated with taking time off.

Set your items to publish with engaging content that does not require a response from your business (unless of course you have someone to monitor the responses). Ensure that you schedule for the high-frequency times of day to hit the highest audience possible. (See Chapter 6 Marketing Online).

Consider also having a voice mail operator who will personally take messages and inform customers of your out of-office status.

***

THE REAL REALITY

Okay, so we have established that you need a time out and ways to successfully do so, but we do need to chit chat for a second about the real reality of taking time off. The real reality is you need it. The real reality is also that not all customers will be so understanding. The real reality is that business opportunities may not wait for you.

Being out of office may result in lost business opportunities, as one may enter your inbox while you're out. Or a customer may be one of those outliers and demand one-hundred percent attention one-hundred percent of the time. However, despite these negatives, the positives are extremely beneficial. Just put into place all appropriate supports, make detailed plans and get some rest. A weary and tired business owner is an unproductive business owner, parent and partner. Sacrificing business for family is a given. The families of small business owners sacrifice a lot. There comes a time when the business must sacrifice a little. Obviously, a smart and strategic business owner and parent will know when too much sacrifice is given on either side. Always keep your eye open for telltale signs of when the family is taking the greatest hit.

Laundry Tip: Loyal customers are the customers you want. Understanding customers are the ones you want. Let the high-maintenance ones go, as they will suck the life and

money out of you. Instead, replace them with loyal and valued customers.

CHAPTER 10:

NOT LOSING YOU

All of this family and business stuff starts with you, so it is imperative that you don't lose yourself in the process. If you take time to implement the efficiency and balancing measures in this book, you'll find more of yourself than you realized; more pleasure in running a business, being a mom and in life itself. It is so easy to get sucked into the boss role (and all other roles that come along with it) and the parenting role that you often forget about yourself.

You probably have heard horror stories of workaholic parents who are never seen at Little Timmy's school play or Little Sally's ballet recital without a smartphone in hand...or the parent who is so overworked their hair is reminiscent of Einstein's and paired with crazy eyes from exhaustion.

Don't be that parent.

Don't turn yourself into a zombie, unless you plan on auditioning for Walking Dead. Seriously, let's not do it. Let's figure out how to stay a normal, functioning and prospering small business owner and parent.

***

STAY FIT

Just like a vehicle or computer, your body needs routine maintenance and checkups. Being fit and dedicating time to working out regularly, eating healthy and getting a full night of sleep will pay dividends in energy, stress and emotional levels. More often than not, it feels like you have absolutely no time. Hopefully by now you've implemented some efficiency measures to balance it all so you can include exercise and healthy meals in your daily routine.

Working Out

Trust me, you can find time to fit it into your schedule to work out. In fact, here's another great tip: depending on what type of exerciser you are, I have found that I do my best brainstorming while working out (or in the shower, but that's a whole another section that we probably won't discuss).

Whether you exercise in the early morning, during your lunch hour or squeeze in an extra hour of flexible time, the benefits of working out will far outweigh any inconvenience you have scheduling the time. Remember all that talk about working on the go? You totally can answer emails via phone while on the stair climber!

Laundry Tip: Even a 20-minute video a day is better than nothing.

Finding time to work out can be especially difficult if you are a single parent or just don't have time to do so without children around.

After the birth of my second daughter I felt sluggish. Lazy. And out of sorts. I wasn't sleeping well (when she let me sleep) and it was affecting the productivity of my business. I knew something had to change. I ordered an at-home video exercise, set up the baby gate to my room and did my workout. I wish I could include a picture, I'd have the two older kids standing at the gate watching me as I worked out. Awkward but I saw the benefits.

Another alternative is to have a personal trainer come to the office to squeeze in a short workout. With the plethora of workout programs online, disc, or in books these days there is no reason you can't find something to fit your schedule.

Eating Right

Here is a good time to plug saving money and eating right. Pre-planning meals is probably one of the last things you want to think about, but can pay off greatly for your pocketbook and hips.

Laundry Tip: Keep healthy snacks available in desk drawers to curb impulse purchases or grabbing of unhealthy snacks.

If you find that you have absolutely no time, consider getting in contact with a local restaurant that can provide deliveries of healthy meals right to the office. Although, I do suggest getting out of the office a few times a day for a quick refresher. You may as well eat while you're at it!

Sleep Schedule

If all else fails, invest in a couch for your office and schedule in power naps for the afternoon. Just be sure to lock your door and set an alarm. It also wouldn't hurt to keep makeup or hair products around in case you wake up looking a hot mess. I have even found myself napping in the car outside of the office just to squeeze in a few minutes. This was especially true during the months of teething or a downright toddler sleep strike.

Laundry Tip: Have set sleep hours. Commit to them as though they were work hours.

Keep in mind that not only will you reap physical and mental benefits, but you will also save money on the insurance front. A healthier you is a lower insurance premium for self-employment insurance!

***

SOCIALIZE

As human beings, socialization is a cornerstone of health and well-being. Just simply going out to socialize will help add some normalcy to life and provide some hours during which you can forget about the long to-do list waiting for you the next day.

Working at home

If your workspace is in-home this is especially important. Some in-home workspace business owners find themselves in a rut that can lead to anxiety or depressed feelings. If you do work in-home, force yourself into socializing even if you are unable to leave. Get up and get dressed as though you were going to an out-of-home office. Keep this routine everyday whether meeting with a customer or staying in the confines of your home office.

Working out-of-home

Even those that retreat out of the recesses of their home to an office everyday aren't immune to the need for socialization. Being in the confines of a sterile office, no matter how awesome your interior decorating skills may be, can slowly suck the life out of anyone if there are not alternative methods of brain stimulation (read: socialization).

Socializing with loved ones

Individuals with partners and/or close friends need (not should, but need) to get out regularly by themselves. No talk of kids, work, obligations. Just take the time to reconnect. I would even go so far as to say that the cost of a babysitter and the reconnecting time should be included in the cost of running the business. Without taking time to reconnect, you can get sucked into a downward spiral of only discussing business (family or real business) and wake up one day to find that stressors are impeding on every area of life. Ward this off with these scheduled times.

Even if you're tired or don't feel like it.

Tough. Go do it.

(That is probably the best Laundry Tip in this book!)

At the end of your life, you won't wish you had responded to that one customer email quicker. You will wish you had spent more time with your loved ones. These evenings don't even have to take an extensive amount of money to accomplish. Merely waiting until the children are in bed to pop open a bottle of wine, order pizza and watch a $1 movie rental fits the bill. Literally. *So give it a try and when you see the results you can thank me with coffee, cookies or high fives on social media!*

***

BE CONFIDENT

Your confidence is probably one of the only tools that no one else can have. Everyone else can have the same product, service and market until end of time...but they cannot recreate you and your confidence.

What is confidence about anyways?

If you are not confident in yourself, why should you expect customers to be confident in your abilities, products or services? You are the most important tool to your company and should demonstrate confidence in yourself and what you are selling. The problem is that many business owners think they *are* confident merely because they went into business. And you may be confident. But if you are not diligent and conscious of sharing this with your audience and they miss it...then what? You may as well have no confidence at all.

Laundry Tip: Be sure you are coming across as confident. Not cocky or superior.

How can I be confident?

When working in industries that require person-to-person interaction, confidence can be exuded through being knowledgeable about the company's offerings, making eye contact and showing genuine interest in the customer's needs. Being knowledgeable shows not only confidence, but also that you have the capabilities to fulfill the customer's demands by being able to provide and educate the customer with information. When a business owner or employee fails to understand the business as a whole or falls short on delivering information, a customer perceives the business as incompetent or not the right fit for them.

Also, it is no surprise that eye contact exudes confidence and initiates a relationship with another person. Relationships with customers are more important than the cash passing between hands. Relationships build a confidence from customer to business owner and a higher probability of returning customers and referrals.

To be confident you should surround yourself with supportive networks, which can include other business owners, family members or social friends. The confidence in yourself and your business can be propelled forward through education and training about running a business and the type of industry you are engaged in. You also can improve your confidence by thinking confidently. The more you want to be confident and the more you work at it, the more likely you are to be confident.

What do I do if I am confident?

Celebrate your achievements. Show humility and gratitude to those around you. **Small businesses are not built by themselves.** Kind of like the whole "it takes a village to raise a child" idea about parenthood, that is also extremely true with businesses. You *can* try to do it on your own but trust me, it helps so much more to balance everything if you give a little and allow others to help. Even if they are just being cheerleaders and sounding boards.

***

EVALUATE WHO YOU'VE BECOME

Have you become a better person? Worse? Scatterbrained? What has the business done to you? Who do you want to be? Whew. That pretty much sums this up...kidding. Start with those questions and identify if your business starts to change you. Is it for the better? Or is it for the worse? Changing for the negative will also detrimentally impact the interpersonal relationships around you.

BIG Laundry Tip: Take it from me; no valued relationship is worth losing due to business.

This should be self-evident, but losing you means you're no longer there. For many, the main reason in starting your own business was so that YOU could be in charge. So YOU could do what YOU wanted. YOU were in control of your career. By losing yourself that YOU is no longer there.

***

And lastly, especially if you start losing you

...GET OUT OF DODGE!

Your schedule will be 24/7 if you don't gain control. This does not mean you should be available 24/7 to everyone. This includes family. You sometimes need to take time for you. Turn off the phone, Internet, and any other communication outlets. Put those carrier pigeons in their cages if you are so concerned about missing a customer inquiry that you actually have those...

Laundry Tip: Even shutting yourself in the broom closet or bathroom for two minutes of sanity is worth it. Your business will not collapse due to a few minutes of absence, but it might if you don't take a breather.

Find time in your schedule to spend time alone, whether it is by hiking, going to the bookstore, hitting the spa, or merely sitting on your bed staring at the ceiling.

Just find you.

AUTHOR BIO

Rachel Brenke is a lawyer, business consultant, and photographer who has developed *The Laundry List* as a real-life, practical guide to assist small business owning moms to successfully reach their business goals while maintaining family.

This book describes how her experiences inspired the consulting business that she runs today. Her writings document her journey to build multiple businesses while balancing three children, graduate school and a deployed military spouse.

Rachel teaches step-by-step approaches to perfecting the balance of family and business. Pulling from her law degree and MBA, she outlines educational theories in plain language and provides real world examples. She is known for her witty blog posts and easy-to-understand approaches to implementing business efficiency measures into a variety of industries.

She also lives in El Paso, Texas with her three children, Army husband and a dog named Archer.

Check out Rachel on the web:
www.rachelbrenke.com
www.facebook.com/rachelbrenke2
www.twitter.com/rachelbrenke
www.thelawtog.com

BASIC BUSINESS PLAN EXAMPLE

Introduction

It is the mission of Rachel Brenke Photography, LLC dba The Law Tog ("RBP)" to provide comprehensive business and marketing consulting for the photography industry. It is our long-term vision and goal to become the go-to and preferred consulting company for photographers internationally. Rachel Brenke believes in creating a long-term working relationship with each client so that implementation of all strategies are founded on in depth understanding of the business and cohesiveness of all actions taken by that company.

The Company

RBP is a limited liability company registered in the State of Texas. Its founder, CEO and primary consultant is Mrs. Rachel Brenke, a former financial analyst for the United States Marine Corps. Mrs. Brenke has brought a variety of educational degrees and industry experiences.

The Services

The company offers services ranging from web-based courses, one-to-one consulting, and products to assist photographers in running their businesses.

Products include:

- Legal Forms
- Marketing Templates
- Workflow charts
- eBooks

- Tutorial videos

The web-based courses offer one-to-one feedback on predesigned assignments submitted in response to lessons.

The one-to-one consulting services may be done via skype, phone or in-person and are ask-all sessions for anything business or marketing related.

The Market

RBP will be concentrating on photographers newly entered into market or established photographers seeking to move forward. This is because these photographers have the greatest need for business consultants. Furthermore, due to photography being an unregulated industry there are few barriers to entry which results in small business owners overwhelmed and seeking assistance.

Financial Considerations

Start-up assets required are $XX,XXX. The CODB is $XXXX yearly and $XXX monthly. RBP will not have outside financers to assist in the finances. At this time, RBP has no intention of seeking financing.

<Insert all costs of doing business + start up costs>

The company has reached profitability since Year 2 and expects to increase growth XX% in Year 3.

Objectives

RBP has the following objectives for the calendar year of 2013.

- A one-year goal for RBP is to increase profitability by XX%.
- Publish a book for mothers seeking small business help

- ○ Establish a minimum of XX% client satisfaction.
- ○ Increase word-of-mouth marketing.
- ○ Establish an online subscription service to educational videos.

Time Line Goals

- 1st Quarter – XXX
- 2nd Quarter – XXX
- 3rd Quarter – XXX
- 4th Quarter - XXX

Keys to Success

RBP's long term survivability and profitability will result due to

- ○ Providing a specialized niche in the photography industry
- ○ Maintain a close rapport with clients and establish future potential relationship needs

Pricing Strategy

RBP will adopt a skimming pricing strategy as the specialized services are in demand with few resources to fulfill the demand.

- Legal Forms $XXX
- Marketing Templates $XX
- Consulting Services $XXX
- Web-based education (course) $XXX
- Web-based education (subscription) $XX/month

Each product will increase by $XX per quarter. Each service will increase by $XXX per quarter. To accompany the increase in price additional value will be created through packaging of products and increased service time.

<u>Marketing Campaigns</u>

RBP will market with the follow campaigns on the designated time table

- January – Kick Off The New Year Webinar + Promotion
- April – Tax Refund Promotion
- July – Mid Year Business Analysis Webinar + Promotion
- October – Preparing For End of Year
- December – Last Minute Tax Purchases Webinar + Promotion

AUTOMATION RESOURCES

Social Media and Blog Publishing

- Hootsuite - www.hootsuite.com
- Twitter Feed - www.twitterfeed.com
- Pingraphy – www.pingraphy.com

Newsletter/Email Automation

- Mailchimp – www.mailchimp.com
- Madmimi - www.madmimi.com
- Aweber – www.aweber.com

Cloud Back Ups

- Backblaze – www.backblaze.com
- Crash Plan – www.crashplan.com
- Dropbox – www.dropbox.com

BLOG PLATFORMS

- Blogger – www.blogger.com
- Wordpress – www.wordpress.com or www.wordpress.org
- Weebly – www.weebly.com
- Squarespace – www.squarespace.com

- Blog – www.blog.com
- Tumblr – www.tumblr.com
- Live Journal – www.livejournal.com

OUTSOURCING RESOURCE LIST

- ODesk – www.odesk.com
- Elance – www.elance.com
- AssistU – www.assistu.com
- VA Networking - www.vanetworking.com
- Guru – www.guru.com

SOCIAL MEDIA RESOURCES

- Twitter – www.twitter.com
- Facebook – www.facebook.com
- Youtube – www.youtube.com
- LinkedIn- www.linkedin.com
- Google+ - http://plus.google.com

LEGAL DISCLAIMER

The information provided in this book is not legal advice. The Laundry List is not a document of a law firm and is not a substitute for an attorney or law firm. The information contained herein is for general use. The Laundry List is providing any kind of advice, explanation, opinion, or recommendation to a consumer about possible legal rights, remedies, defenses, options, selection of forms or strategies.

Made in the USA
San Bernardino, CA
13 June 2016